T0044989

What Do We Owe
to Refugees?

Political Theory Today series

David Owen

—————

What Do We Owe to Refugees?

polity

First published in 2020 by Polity Press

Polity Press
65 Bridge Street
Cambridge CB2 1UR, UK

Polity Press
101 Station Landing
Suite 300
Medford, MA 02155, USA

ISBN-13: 978-1-5095-3973-4
ISBN-13: 978-1-5095-3974-1(pb)

A catalogue record for this book is available from the British Library.

Library of Congress Cataloging-in-Publication Data
Names: Owen, David, 1964- author.
Title: What do we owe to refugees? / David Owen.
Description: Cambridge, UK ; Medford, MA : Polity Press, 2020. | Series: Political theory today | Includes bibliographical references and index. | Summary: "Who are refugees? Who, if anyone, is responsible for protecting them? What forms should this protection take? In this engaging and concise book, David Owen provides a clear account of the responsibilities of refugee protection and the forms of international co-operation that will be required to discharge them"-- Provided by publisher.
Identifiers: LCCN 2019025264 | ISBN 9781509539734 (hardback) | ISBN 9781509539741 (paperback) | ISBN 9781509539758 (epub)
Subjects: LCSH: Refugees. | Emigration and immigration--International cooperation. | Emigration and immigration--Government policy.
Classification: LCC HV640 .O89 2020 | DDC 325/.21--dc23
LC record available at https://lccn.loc.gov/2019025264

Typeset in 11 on 15 Sabon by Servis Filmsetting Ltd, Stockport, Cheshire
Printed and bound in Great Britain by CPI Group (UK) Ltd, Croydon

For further information on Polity, visit our website: politybooks.com

Contents

To Miranda

With the hope that your generation will do better

Acknowledgements

I have accumulated many debts over the years; the main ones are to Liza Schuster, who introduced me to the issue, to Matt Gibney, from whom I have learnt most (perhaps not enough), and to Joseph Carens and Rainer Bauböck, who have each critically supported my thinking about this topic. Others whose thinking and comments have helped me along the way include Alex Aleinikoff, Sarah Fine, David Miller, Kelly Oliver, Clara Sandelind, James Souter, Christine Straehle, Kerri Woods and Leah Zamore. Particular thanks are due to Chris Armstrong, Chris Bertram, Peter Niesen, Anne Phillips and Tracy Strong, for responses to the whole manuscript.

I was fortunate to have the political philosophy group at the University of Milan devote a workshop to the draft manuscript, and I am grateful to Corrado Fumagalli for organising it and to his colleagues for their critical insights. Special thanks are due to Gloria Zuccarelli and Laura Santi Amantini for detailed and helpful comments on the manuscript and to Valeria Ottonelli for raising an important point I had not adequately considered. I am also grateful to George Owers and Julia Davies at Polity, who have been exemplary throughout the process, and to two anonymous reviewers.

Outside academic life I owe a debt to two friends – Jon Courtenay Grimwood and Simon Nicholson – who read the manuscript of this book as fellow writers, with an ear to its accessibility to the lay reader. My wife, Caroline Wintersgill, has offered her always steadfast love and support (even while trying to finish her PhD); and our children, Miranda and Arthur, sustain me in more ways than they know. Because I admire her passionate concern for justice, I dedicate this book to Miranda.

Prologue

A Tale of Two Ships

Let me begin with two stories.

The first is the tale of the German ocean liner MS *St Louis*, which departed from Hamburg on 13 May 1939 carrying 937 passengers; nearly all of them were Jews fleeing Nazi Germany. The passengers had, for the most part, already applied for US visas and had landing permits or transit visas for Cuba, where they intended to disembark and wait for visas to enter the United States. It was a two-week transatlantic voyage and the trip was pleasant, offering music, dance and Friday night prayers (during which the portrait of Adolf Hitler was removed from the dining room). Unknown to the passengers, their voyage had already attracted considerable media attention in Cuba: 'Even before the ship sailed from Hamburg, right-wing Cuban newspapers deplored its impending arrival and demanded that the Cuban government cease admitting Jewish refugees.'[1] The director general of the Cuban Immigration Office was forced to resign over the illegal sale of landing permits, and in the week before the ship sailed the Cuban president issued a decree 'that invalidated all recently issued landing certificates'.[2] Refugees from Europe were portrayed by right-wing populist movements as threatening Cubans' economic security by taking scarce jobs away from natives.[3] When the St Louis arrived at Havana on 27 May, only 28 passengers (22 of whom were Jewish) were held to have valid papers and allowed to disembark – alongside one other, who tried to commit suicide and was hospitalised in Havana.

The fate of the passengers on the St Louis was now a major story in newspapers across Europe and the Americas. Appeals to the US government were made to no avail. The United States operated a quota system for immigration that was based on the size of existing US population groups; and the combined German Austrian quota of 27,370 for 1939 not only was filled, but left a long waiting list. Moreover, there was no political will to admit higher numbers:

A Fortune Magazine poll at the time indicated that 83 percent of Americans opposed relaxing restrictions on immigration. President Roosevelt could have issued an executive order to admit the *St Louis* refugees, but this general hostility to immigrants, the gains of isolationist Republicans in the Congressional elections of 1938, and Roosevelt's consideration of running for an unprecedented third term as president were among the political considerations that militated against taking this extraordinary step in an unpopular cause.[4]

With no other choice available, on 6 June the *St Louis* set sail to return to Europe. The worst fear of the passengers was a return to Germany, but the Jewish Joint Distribution Committee (alongside other Jewish organisations) was able to use its funds to arrange visas to four other European states: Great Britain (288), France (224), Belgium (214) and the Netherlands (181). The passengers admitted to Great Britain were the lucky ones, as only one was killed during the war in an air raid; of those trapped on the continent, 87 manged to leave Europe again before the German invasion in 1940, but 532 did not – and 254 were killed in the Holocaust: '84 who had been in Belgium; 84 who had found refuge in Holland, and 86 who had been admitted to France'.[5]

The second story is that of the MV *Aquarius*, run by SOS Méditerranée and Médecins Sans

Frontières. Since 2016, this ship operated as a search-and-rescue vessel for asylum seekers and migrants in danger of drowning in the crossing from Libya to Europe, working in cooperation with the Italian Maritime Rescue Coordination Centre. On 10 June 2018, Matteo Salvini, the interior minister of Italy's newly formed right-wing populist government, refused permission for *Aquarius* to dock with 629 rescued persons (including 123 unaccompanied minors, 11 younger children and seven pregnant women). Salvini claimed, contrary to the international law of rescue at sea, that Malta rather than Italy should accept those rescued – a demand that Malta vehemently rejected. Buoyed by popular support in Italy for a tough anti-immigrant policy, Salvini maintained his refusal, proclaiming that 'Italy was saying "no to human trafficking, no to the business of illegal immigration"'.[6] The stand-off was resolved only when Spain gave permission for *Aquarius* to dock in Valencia and agreed to accept those rescued persons on board. Italy's actions took place against the background of economic austerity that followed the effects of the 2008 financial crash and the emergence or consolidation of right-wing national populist movements in the EU, as well as the failure of the Common European Asylum System to secure fair refugee responsibility sharing across its member states, a failure that had seen frontline states such as Italy under particular pressure.

After these events *Aquarius* encountered further problems. First Gibraltar and, next, Panama, perhaps under pressure from the Italian government, revoked the registration it required to operate under their flag. In November 2018 Italian prosecutors, somewhat arbitrarily, ordered the seizure of the *Aquarius* to investigate charges that it had illegally dumped potentially hazardous waste at Italian ports (a charge rejected by SOS Méditerranée and Médecins Sans Frontières); the effect of this order was to deny *Aquarius* access to Italian waters. Such measures increased the pressure on the inadequately resourced Libyan coastguard at a time when the death toll from attempted crossings was, not coincidentally, at its highest in history. On 7 December, having been stranded in Marseille since early October, the *Aquarius* officially ceased operations with Médecins Sans Frontières, blaming this on 'sustained attacks on search and rescue by European states'.[7] During this period of stasis, an estimated 389 persons seeking to cross the Mediterranean have drowned, although the figure may well be higher.[8] (It is likely that, by the time this book is published, things will have got worse, given the deteriorating situation in Libya.)

While the contexts in which these two sets of events took place are different, there are significant parallels, notably that, under conditions of economic austerity, potentials for national hostility towards people seeking refuge were mobilised by right-wing populist actors, cultivated for domestic political advantage and made to support restrictive policies against those in flight. However, whereas the story of the *St Louis* may be seen as one of far too many that contributed to motivating the establishment of the international refugee regime in the aftermath of the genocidal murders and mass displacements of the Second World War, the story of the *Aquarius* speaks to the contemporary limitations of this regime, in particular in securing international cooperation between states and safe passage for refugees. It is against the background of such stories that the question of what is owed to refugees and how their protection can be secured acquires its ethical urgency and its political salience.

Introduction

We commit to a more equitable sharing of the burden and responsibility for hosting and supporting the world's refugees.

New York Declaration for Refugees and Migrants (2016)

Today, as people flee civil wars, authoritarian states, persecution by state and non-state actors, famine and environmental disaster, the international refugee regime that was forged in the aftermath of global war and extended in the context of the independence struggles and post-independence conflicts of the second half of the twentieth century is creaking, perhaps cracking, under the strain. The images that we see, of overcrowded boats crossing the Mediterranean and drowned bodies washed up on Europe's holidays beaches, or of caravans of displaced people trekking to the Mexican border with the United States – and the images that we generally don't see, of people dying in desert crossings in Libya and Mexico, or of families warehoused in refugee camps across Africa and Asia[1] – have led the UN secretary general to speak of a global crisis of solidarity. Many in need of protection do not receive it, and even those who reach camps (or urban spaces) often fail to find security.[2]

Acknowledgement of the failings of our current political framework for responding to refugee crises and the need for a renewed approach to refugee protection found expression in the United Nations' 2016 New York Declaration for Refugees and Migrants, which highlighted the need for greater international cooperation and responsibility sharing.[3] But what exactly is the nature of the responsibility that states owe to refugees? And what kinds of international cooperation are required? To raise these questions is to ask how we should approach refugee protection today. Who should count as a refugee and what is owed to persons with that status? Is it sufficient for the international community to provide funds to meet the basic humanitarian needs of refugees in the (typically neighbouring) states of immediate refuge? What weight should be given to the refugees' own choices – exhibited, for example, in embarking on dangerous journeys to Europe or the

United States? Under what conditions can refugees be repatriated to their own states? These are among the most pressing ethical questions in contemporary politics and it is the task of this book to provide a framework for addressing them.

One pragmatic response to these questions can be found in the Global Compact on Refugees, a non-binding agreement that the New York Declaration tasked the United Nations High Commissioner for Refugees (UNHCR) with drafting.[4] Its objectives are to ease pressures on host countries and to expand access to the resettlement of refugees in other states, as well as to enhance refugee self-reliance and support conditions in countries of origin for the safe return of refugees. The adoption of this compact is a significant diplomatic achievement, although the challenge of securing the voluntary cooperation among the relevant actors that is required for implementing the compact will be considerably more demanding. But, if we are to evaluate responses to the contemporary predicaments of refugee protection, we need to step back from our immediate political context and engage in a deeper investigation of the institution of refugeehood.

Such a project is necessary not simply because the established refugee regime is under strain as a result of failures of international cooperation. One reason why it is necessary is, more fundamentally, that the figure of the refugee in contemporary politics (as well as in academic literature) is caught between two distinct and incompatible pictures of refugeehood – humanitarian and political – that give rise to rather different accounts of who is entitled to refugee status, of the obligations owed to refugees, and of the appropriate international organisation of refugee protection.

Two Pictures of Refugees

The *humanitarian* picture identifies refugees as forcibly displaced persons who have typically crossed an international border – that is, people who have a compelling reason to flee, or not to return to, their home state on the grounds that return would pose a threat to their basic needs. This picture of refugees and our relationship to them 'pervades the public imagination and academic literature':

> The term 'refugee' connotes people fleeing war, famine, and failed states. They are portrayed as victims waiting in camps until they can return or be resettled. These are the 'neediest' of the needy such that 'a refugee's plight appears morally tantamount to that of a baby who has been left on one's door-

step in the dead of winter'. Characterizations like this represent what has been called a 'humanitarian' conception of refugees where a foreigner's need for protection – regardless of whether that need results from persecution, civil war, famine, extreme poverty, or some other cause – grounds a claim for asylum. The more serious and urgent is the need for protection, the stronger is that claim.[5]

A clear example of the humanitarian picture is provided by Betts and Collier in their recent book *Refuge: Transforming a Broken Refugee System*, where they argue that 'Syrians forced to flee their homes by violence' are ethically analogous to a 'drowning child' and 'we have an unambiguous duty of rescue towards them'.[6]

By contrast, the *political* picture argues for the distinctiveness of refugees by comparison to other forced migrants:

> Refugees are special because persecution is a special harm. Refugees 'are targeted for harm in a manner that repudiates their claim to political membership'; their 'rights go unprotected because they are unrecognized' rather than for other reasons. . . . Refugees are distinctive because their country of origin has effectively repudiated their membership and the protection it affords. The status on which almost all their other rights hinge is gone.[7]

This picture draws a sharp distinction between refugees and what Michael Walzer calls 'necessitous strangers':

> Both are distinct from [voluntary] immigrants. Necessitous strangers are 'destitute and hungry' people fleeing generalized catastrophes. Their needs can be met 'by yielding territory' or 'exporting wealth' while withholding membership. Yet refugees are 'victims of . . . persecution' whose 'need is for membership itself, a non-exportable good'.[8]

Whereas 'necessitous strangers' require humanitarian aid, refugees require asylum. The humanitarian and the political pictures of refugeehood thus diverge in their responses to the question of who should be entitled to refugee status; so, for example, from the humanitarian perspective there is no essential moral difference between people fleeing persecution and people fleeing famine, or between those who flee across international borders and those who are forcibly displaced within their state of nationality, whereas from the political perspective only persons outside the state and threatened by persecution should be entitled to refugeehood. Even more, the two pictures also shape distinct understandings of what obligations are owed to persons with that status; and these understandings, in turn, have significant implications for how such obligations should be shared and for how we think about the nature of the grant of refugee status as an expressive act. For the humanitarian picture, the underlying obligation is a *moral duty to prevent undeserved suffering*; this obligation takes the form of providing a refuge within which basic needs can be secured and protected as long as the costs of doing so are not unreasonably burdensome. Hence the focus of international cooperation is on *sharing the burden of protecting refugees from serious harm*, while the act of granting refuge (and of providing resources for refugee protection) is a communicative act that expresses *moral solidarity* with vulnerable strangers. By contrast, for the political picture, the underlying obligation is a *political obligation to redress the injustice of membership repudiation to which refugees are subject*; this obligation takes the form of providing refugees with asylum, which is conceived of as 'surrogate membership' in a state that is not their own, and thereby reasserting their political standing as equal members of global political society. Hence the focus of international cooperation is on *sharing the responsibility of upholding the political standing of persons whose membership has been wrongfully repudiated*, while the act of granting asylum is a

7

communicative act that expresses *political condemnation* of the persecuting state.

The dilemma constructed by the coexistence of these different pictures is both political and philosophical. It is political, first, because it generates ethical indeterminacy concerning *who* should count as a 'genuine' refugee, and this indeterminacy is often exploited by politicians and media commentators for their own purposes. Second, this indeterminacy makes it difficult to hold states politically accountable for their responses to flows of asylum seekers (even if a shared legal definition of 'refugee' is adopted for policy purposes), precisely because both the nature and the extent of their duties are conditional on how the institution of refugeehood is conceived of. Politicians often claim that 'we' have done 'our fair share', but what, if anything, does the appeal to 'fair shares' mean in this context? Consider two facts:

1 In 2018 the UNHCR estimated that there are 25.4 million refugees worldwide and a further 3.1 million asylum seekers whose claims have not yet been assessed, and that 85 per cent of the world's refugees are hosted in the developing world (Turkey, Uganda, Pakistan, Lebanon and Iran being the top hosting states), while only

102,800 refugees were granted resettlement places (typically in the developed world).[9]

2   The major funders of the UNHCR are the United States, the EU, individual states in the developed world (including those in the EU), oil-rich Gulf states, and private donors based in developed world states.[10]

Does this represent an unfair division of responsibility for refugee protection? On the one hand, the developed world takes in a relatively low percentage of the world's refugee population under the UNHCR's definition – one that has declined from about 25 per cent to about 15 per cent over roughly the last decade.[11] Indeed, many of the states of the developed world have spent the past 30–40 years deploying non-entry policies designed to prevent those who seek refuge from reaching their borders in order to claim asylum, while offering little in the way of resettlement places.[12] On the other hand, these same states and their citizens provide the overwhelming bulk of funding for the UNHCR as the primary agency of refugee protection. How, then, should 'fair shares' be determined? On the basis of numbers of refugees admitted? On the basis of contributions to the costs of protection? By reference to the wealth of states? Answering such questions requires a determinate account of who is entitled to refugeehood, of what is owed to refugees, and of what norms should govern a fair scheme of international cooperation; but this is precisely what is lacking.[13] In the absence of an adequate account of the institution of refugeehood, the appeal to 'fair shares' lacks any determinate content and cannot underwrite domestic, international or transnational processes of holding states accountable with respect to refugee protection. This lack of determinacy is no doubt part of its rhetorical appeal.

The dilemma created by the coexistence of the two distinct pictures of refugees is also philosophical. It is so for the obvious reason that it raises the challenge of working out an adequate normative account of refugeehood in the face of two contrasting and incompatible views. But the challenge is philosophically deeper than that because, if it is to be satisfying, such an account must also make sense of the grip that these two pictures have established on our ethical and political imaginations. How, then, should we take up this challenge? The guiding thought of this book is that this task is best accomplished by providing a normative reconstruction of the point and purpose of the institution of refugeehood that is grounded in attention to the historical emergence and development of this institution and to the conditions of political legitimacy of the international order of states within which the institution of refugeehood is situated.[14] The book's hope is that such an account will enable us to make sense of how we have reached our current predicament, to understand the inadequacies of both pictures, and to provide an alternative view, which should enable us to return to the ethical and political challenges of refugee protection with a renewed understanding of the ground, justification and value of the international refugee regime – and of what it requires of us. The argument unfolds across four chapters.

Structure of the Book

The first chapter begins with an historical overview of the making of the modern refugee regime that aims to make sense of the grip that the humanitarian and political pictures of refugeehood hold on us by tracking their roots and the practical interactions between them. This historical reconstruction of the modern refugee regime provides the basis for the second chapter, which offers a conceptual reconstruction of the normative function of the institution of refugeehood that aims to move beyond the humanitarian–political opposition. Central to this account is the role of this institution in relation to the conditions of political legitimacy of the international order of states. Refugees, it is argued, are people for whom the international community must stand *in loco civitatis*, that is, as a substitute for their own state.[15] What this relationship demands, it is proposed, can vary according to whether refugees require asylum, sanctuary, or refuge. The first is exemplified by the case of the people who have reasonable grounds to fear persecution by their home state (or by non-state actors from which their state is unwilling to offer protection); the second, by people fleeing generalised violence and the breakdown of civil order; the third, by people fleeing specific state failures such as famine or natural disasters such as floods (where the line between 'state failure' and 'natural disaster' is typically blurred). The argument distinguishes general obligations owed to all refugees and particular obligations owed to each of these three types of refugee.

In chapter 3 I turn from this conceptual reconstruction of the normative function of the institution of refugeehood to the question of responsibility for refugees, of *who* owes *what* to *whom*. This chapter may be viewed as an exercise in 'ideal theory', in the specific sense that it aims to lay out the responsibilities that states *ought* to acknowledge and act on, independently of their willingness to do so. Here I address the different responsibilities owed to each of the three types of refugees and their implications for the sharing of overall responsibility for refugees, before turning to consider the criteria that should govern the allocation of responsibility for refugee protection. The final chapter returns to reflection on the current refuge regime – its limitations and challenges – in a world in which many states don't generally comply with their obligations. It asks what factors help to explain this non-compliance and considers how compliance might be encouraged, before turning to ask what implications this condition has for the duties of the international community, of non-cooperating states, of their citizens, and of refugees.

1

Picturing Refugees

Forced Displacement and the Making of the
Modern Refugee Regime

Practices of asylum, sanctuary and refuge have a long history; but their distinctive political form in our contemporary world is shaped by the emergence, and eventual global spread, of an international order of sovereign territorial states. Refugees are, as Haddad puts it, the practically unavoidable result 'of erecting boundaries, attempting to assign all individuals to a territory within such boundaries, and then failing to ensure universal representation and protection'.[1] The focus in this chapter is on the emergence and development of the modern refugee regime, that is, on sketching the lines of descent that coalesce in the two pivotal institutions that make up this regime – the 1951 Refugee Convention and the 1950 United Nations High Commissioner for Refugees (UNHCR) – and the development of this regime in the changing contexts of post-war global politics. In short, this chapter aims to show how we arrived at the contemporary refugee regime and how this path has led to the grip that the two contrasting pictures of refugees, humanitarian and political, have on our ethical imaginations.

Lines of Descent: Persecution, Humanitarianism and Multilateralism

On 22 October 1685 Louis XIV issued the Edict of Fontainebleau. This proclamation, which followed a series of earlier repressive measures directed at the Reformed Protestant (Calvinist) population in France, revoked the 1598 Edict of Nantes, through which Henri IV had granted religious liberty to those nicknamed 'Huguenots' by their enemies. The new edict forbade Reformed Protestant religious services and required the exile of pastors who would not recant their faith, but at the same time denied the laity the right to leave France. Louis had compelling reasons to forbid the emigration of the Huguenots, who comprised a highly skilled portion of the French workforce. Despite the denial of sovereign permission to leave France, an estimated 200,000 Huguenots fled to Protestant states such as Denmark, England, Holland and Prussia.

The French policy was not only a threat to its Huguenot population; it also posed a challenge to the norms that marked out the minimal conditions of peaceful coexistence in a religiously fractured Europe and that, after years of violent conflict across the continent, had been affirmed in the Peace of Westphalia (1648). Central to these conditions of peaceful coexistence were the extension to the Reformed Protestant Church of the provisions of the Peace of Augsburg (1555) for religious toleration and the reaffirmation of religious minorities' right to emigrate on confessional grounds. Louis XIV's simultaneous denial of even limited religious toleration to the Reformed Protestant Church and of the right to leave France to its faithful thus provided a test of the commitment of an emerging European international society organised around the norm of state sovereignty to the standards of legitimate state conduct that the Peace of Westphalia had endorsed. It presented the Protestant states of Europe with a dilemma: '[H]ow could they accommodate the Huguenots in a way that would express their concerns over Louis XIV's actions but still avoid conflict with France?'[2] What was needed was a way of affirming the normative conditions of peaceful coexistence by condemning French policy as illegitimate that, at the same time, avoided direct conflict with France and reasserted the norm of state sovereignty as the basis of the European political order. This was achieved by creating a distinct category of migrants: 'ones who, because they could no longer count on the protection of their own state, should be allowed to leave that state and receive protection elsewhere'.[3] It is thus that the word 'refugee' enters the English language, from the French word *réfugié*, which was used specifically to describe those Huguenots who fled France. The political picture of the refugee has its modern roots here.

This response to persons fleeing religious persecution was extended within broadly European-based international society to those who faced political persecution in the context of persons fleeing the American and French Revolutions, before it was further adapted and refined in nineteenth-century debates about asylum and non-extradition.[4] These two revolutions made new normative resources central to European-based international society – namely the rights of man and popular sovereignty – and these shaped political understandings of the limits on legitimate state conduct towards its citizens in ways that were important to the concept of refugees and to the norm of asylum; but they also introduced a sharpening of the legal distinction between citizens and aliens and its social realisation as a contrast between nationals and foreigners that would become increasingly politically salient at the century's end. The French Revolution also produced what became the archetypical nineteenth-century refugee figure: the political revolutionary. Given the open immigration regime of European-based international society in this period, the norm of granting asylum was less a matter of admission to a state than a matter of protection from return to a persecuting state that sought to extradite the political fugitive. Part of the significance of this development was that, whereas granting asylum to religious refugees was typically grounded in confessional solidarity, this did not apply to asylum granted to political exiles, whose transnational political activity could also be a source of diplomatic tension between states; yet the practice that emerged in the nineteenth century identified the admission and protection of refugees, political or otherwise, as norms that should be respected even where there were prudential reasons not to do so.[5] Within European-based international society, Orchard argues:

States in the nineteenth century held a consistent view of refugees as people fleeing political and religious persecution who should be allowed to leave their own states, who should be offered protection in domestic law, and who should not be returned. ... Although accepting refugees remained the purview of individual states, clear notions of correct behaviour towards refugees shaped the interactions of states with international society, founded in the basic rules established by the fundamental institutions of territoriality, international law, and popular sovereignty.[6]

This informal regime established the basic shape of norms that would be central to the modern refugee regime, but its lack of resilience became clear as the numbers of refugees fleeing persecution grew rapidly in the late nineteenth and early twentieth century and states became increasingly reluctant to admit them.

The norm of protection for persons liable to religious or political persecution by their own state is the source of the political picture of refugees; and the development of this norm is the first of the three lines of descent that will come together to compose the grounds of the modern refugee regime. The second line is rooted in the development of humanitarian organisations in the nineteenth century

– most famously, the founding of the International Committee of the Red Cross (ICRC) in 1863 – and in the large-scale population displacements, including 'voluntary' population exchanges, that accompanied regional instability in the Balkans in the late nineteenth and early twentieth centuries. While the ICRC was focused on the suffering of soldiers in warfare, national and international humanitarian relief efforts were mobilised on behalf of these populations that identified them as refugees. Thus, for example, displaced Muslims who fled to Turkey were housed, in part, in new settlements with names such as Muhacirköy ('Refugee's Village'), while bodies such as the International Committee for the Relief of Turkish Refugees were founded to mobilise humanitarian aid.[7] These developments prefigured the larger population displacements that would occur during and after the First World War and the expansion of organised humanitarianism in terms of both numbers of organisations and scope of the aid that established bodies such as the ICRC and its national committees undertook. With this war, civilians became a central focus of international humanitarianism – and 'refugee' as a term 'became part of the common currency of politics and public opinion'.[8] Its use encompassed not only persons fleeing persecution but, more generally, populations in flight from generalised conditions of violence that posed a serious threat to their safety and well-being. The emergence of the humanitarian picture can be located here. At the same time, to be identified as a 'refugee' in this expanded sense and hence to gain humanitarian assistance meant not only to be subject to a process of bureaucratic assessment but to be represented in ways that had social costs:

> To be labelled a refugee had demeaning consequences, stripping away attributes of social distinction and class to leave oneself [*sic*] exposed to a sense of pure deprivation. The consequences of this silencing are eerily familiar to the modern reader. A Belgian refugee spoke from the heart when he summed up his feeling: 'One was always a refugee – that's the name one was given, a sort of nickname (*sobriquet*). One was left with nothing, ruined, and that's how people carried on talking about "the refugee". We weren't real people anymore.'[9]

In contrast to the earlier picturing of religious and political refugees as persons who are persecuted in virtue of their agency, whose rights are threatened precisely because they are agents exercising their freedom of religious or political expression, the emerging humanitarian picture of the refugee is one of a vulnerable creature exposed to undeserved harm, as the 'victim of unstoppable forces'.[10]

The third and final line of descent emerges in the interwar years, with the 'multilateral' turn to seeing refugee flows as a matter of international concern that requires cooperation between states. The central events in creating the conditions for this turn were the shattering of the Austro-Hungarian and Ottoman empires in the course and aftermath of the First World War, in combination with the Russian Revolution and the consequent Civil War. The latter saw (now stateless) Russians scattered across the globe and, following an approach to the League of Nations by the International Committee of the Red Cross, in September 1921 the explorer Fridtjof Nansen was appointed as League of Nations High Commissioner for Refugees (LNHCR), being granted a temporary mandate to assist 'any person of Russian origin who does not enjoy or who no longer enjoys the protection of the Government of the USSR, and who has not acquired another nationality'.[11]

Notably, it was the case that the ICRC 'in particular emphasized that this assistance should be understood as politically neutral humanitarianism',[12] an understanding that was strengthened by the central role of charitable relief organisations in supporting Nansen's efforts and that would be repeated in relation to the foundation of the

UNHCR. Nansen's mandate was soon extended beyond the case of stateless Russians and made to address new refugee flows, for each of which a new 'arrangement' had to be negotiated.[13] After Nansen's death, there was an attempt to move to a more general multilateral approach with the 1933 Convention Relating to the International Status of Refugees, which, in generalising from the previous 'arrangements' system, was group-based.[14] This was followed by the 1938 Convention Concerning the Status of Refugees Coming from Germany, which shifted to an individualised specification of refugees and introduced the important principle that 'refugees who have been authorised to reside therein may not be subjected by the authorities to measures of expulsion or recondition unless such measures are dictated by reasons of national security or public order'.[15] These came too late.[16] The mass denationalisations of the 1930s and the increasing reluctance of states to admit refugees as domestic concerns about sovereignty and immigration trumped (what was seen as) humanitarian policies overwhelmed the nascent multilateral refugee regime with the tragic consequences symbolised in the voyage of the German ocean liner MS *St Louis*.

These three lines of descent combine to provide a conception of refugees as persons whose claim is predicated on lack of protection from their own state and who are outside that state; on a principle of non-refoulement (i.e. of not being returned to one's own state); on the use of both individualised and group-based determination procedures; on the central role of humanitarian organisations in both advocacy and assistance; and on the importance of multilateral cooperation. They provide the roots of the contrasting political and humanitarian pictures of refugees and the materials from which the modern refugee regime is constructed. Notably, they also illustrate the difficulties of securing multilateral cooperation. The inadequacy of the interwar regime and its consequences offer a stark warning about the costs of the failure of the international community to respond effectively to mass refugee flows.

Constructing the Modern Regime

Significant as they were, the population displacements of the interwar years were dwarfed by those that arose as effects of the Second World War. This gave a new impetus to refugee organisations and led eventually to the establishment of the Office of the UNHCR in 1950, which, although intended as a

24

temporary humanitarian organisation that 'should be a "non-operational" body dependent on voluntary organisations to assist refugees',[17] remains the central international agency for contemporary refugee protection.[18]

Alongside the UNHCR, the other lynchpin of the contemporary refugee regime, as already mentioned, is the 1951 Refugee Convention following the lifting of its original geographic and temporal restrictions through the 1967 Protocol. Prior to the 1967 Protocol, the Convention's scope was limited to persons fleeing events that occurred before 1 January 1951 and within Europe. It was focused on ensuring the resettlement of displaced persons in Europe who had reasonable grounds to fear being returned to their state of nationality (or, if stateless, to their prior habitual residence). The Convention both provides a legal specification or definition of the figure of the refugee and establishes the fundamental norm of the contemporary refugee regime. The definition runs thus:

> One who owing to a well-founded fear of being persecuted for reasons of race, religion, nationality [as belonging to a 'people'], membership of a social group or political opinion is outside the country of his nationality [as membership of a state] and is unable or, owing to such fear, is unwilling to avail

himself of the protection of that country; or who, not having a nationality and being outside the country of his habitual residence . . . is unable, or, owing to such fear, is unwilling to return to it.[19]

The norm is that of non-refoulement. The duty of non-refoulement is a binding obligation, on any state to which a claim to asylum is made, not to return persons who are found to satisfy the criteria of refugeehood to the state from which they have fled or to another state in which they would lack protection.[20] Importantly, the Convention marks out the distinctiveness of refugees not only in terms of a claim to the protection of a state that is not their own but also by positioning the figure of the refugee between that of the citizen and that of the resident non-citizen and by ascribing to refugees some rights that put them on an equal footing with citizens and other rights that make them at least equal to the most favoured among the non-citizen residents. It also ascribes to the state of asylum the duty to ensure that the refugee enjoys the assistance necessary for international travel and protection when abroad that would normally be provided by the refugee's state of nationality.[21]

The relevance of highlighting both the 1951 Convention and the UNHCR is that the former was clearly political in the sense that its focus was on the persecution–membership nexus and it was designed to protect 'the international system of states that is threatened when states fail to fulfil their proper roles',[22] while the role, focus and self-understanding of the latter were primarily humanitarian – and developments in each of these institutions have interacted in ways that highlight the tension between the political and the humanitarian pictures.

As the UNHCR developed from its limited beginnings, its humanitarian self-understanding became increasingly important for the practice of refugee protection. The UNHCR established itself as the central agency of refugee protection through its role in a series of refugee crises that did not easily or directly fall under the scope of the 1951 Convention. While its leadership in responding to the refugee crisis that followed the 1956 Hungarian Revolution was central to establishing it as the most important international organisation for refugee protection, this case already indicated a degree of flexibility in relation to restrictions of the 1951 Convention[23] that would be further developed through the emergence of the 'good offices' extension of its role into Asia and Africa. The 'good offices' extension allowed the UNHCR to expand its remit beyond refugees covered by the 1951 Convention and also saw the range of services that it offered to refugees and host governments widen from basic humanitarian assistance. Initially the 'good offices' extension took a case-by-case form but, echoing the earlier pattern with regard to 'arrangements' in the interwar period, this form was dropped and in 1961 the UN adopted a resolution that gave the High Commissioner for Refugees authority 'to assist both "refugees within his mandate and those for whom he extends his good offices", effectively removing the legal and institutional barriers to future UNHCR action for non-mandate refugees'.[24] Importantly for my concerns, [t]he good offices basis for action contained no assumption of persecution . . . But at the same time the UNHCR disclaimed any intention of seeking a long-term solution to these problems or of assuming ongoing legal protection for these groups.'[25]

In 1965 the UN dropped the distinction between 'mandate' and 'good office' refugees in relation to the UNHCR, requesting that the High Commissioner provide 'protection and permanent solutions to all groups within his competence'.[26] With these developments, the humanitarian picture extends into what had been the domain of the political picture, a development further complicated through the rise of regional refugee conventions.

Awareness that the legal specification of refugees

in the 1951 Convention had been developed for the post-war context in Europe and did not fit well with the pragmatics of forced migration in the developing world led the UNHCR both to push for removal of the temporal and geographic restrictions of the 1951 Convention through the 1967 Protocol and to work with the Organisation of African Unity (OAU) to develop a regional refugee convention – the 1969 OAU Convention Governing the Specific Aspects of Refugee Problems in Africa – that was rooted in acknowledgement of the newly universalised 1951 Convention but extended the scope of refugeehood to cover those fleeing the breakdown of public order and generalised violence in response to the postcolonial African context. These two developments set the stage for the global expansion of the work of the UNHCR over the following decades, major refugee challenges emerging across Asia, Africa, the Americas and Europe along with further regional developments such as the non-binding 1984 Cartagena Declaration after the expansive path set by the OAU to cover Latin America and, most recently, the attempt by the European Union to develop a more restrictive but legally binding Common European Asylum System.

Two key developments that are of central concern for my enquiry relate to the expansion of the

UNHCR's role in relation to displaced persons who remain inside their states of nationality – so-called 'internally displaced persons' (IDPs) and, more recently, in relation to persons who are displaced by 'natural' disasters. These are significant in practical terms – thus, for example, there are an estimated 25.4 million refugees (under the OAU definition) and 40 million IDPs in the world today, and it is estimated that about 25 million people were displaced by weather-related disasters in the last year. But these developments are also intellectually important, because they raise sharply the question of who should be entitled to refugee status and what obligations are owed to persons with that status; and these have been (and remain) matters of central controversy in terms of how we conceive of the point and purpose of the international refugee regime of which the UNHCR is a central part. More specifically, these developments heighten and sharpen the tension between humanitarian and political pictures of refugeehood. From the political standpoint, they represent the progressive erosion of the fundamentally distinct kind of claim that refugees have in comparison to other kinds of necessitous strangers. Thus, for example, in 2007 James Hathaway, a prominent scholar of refugee law, used his keynote address to the International Association for the

Study of Forced Migration to respond to UNHCR's increasingly bold policy concerning IDPs by insisting on the political distinctiveness of refugees.[27] By contrast, from the humanitarian standpoint it is relatively straightforward to see why not only the situation of people who have crossed borders to flee generalised conditions of violence but also that of people who remain within a state characterised by such conditions demands our aid, as long as it is not unreasonably burdensome for us to provide it. Just as the differentiation between those whose lives are endangered by persecution and those whose lives are endangered by the breakdown of public order appears morally arbitrary from this humanitarian perspective, so too does the differential treatment of *either* those outside and inside the state in question *or* those whose lives are threatened by natural disasters rather than by human ones. Moral solidarity demands that we approach all of these persons as having the same kind of claim on us; and, while there may be salient differences in terms of addressing those claims (for example, the dangers of trying to protect persons inside a state engaged in civil war), these are matters relating to the different burdens that may arise in different situations rather than to differences in the kinds of claim made on us. Thus, in a reply to Hathaway's argument, Adelman and

McGrath argue that most refugees under UNHCR protection had fled conflict, not persecution, and that, to the extent that IDPs meet the same criteria, they should be entitled to the same treatment.[28]

These reflections on the developing role of the UNHCR and on the tensions that attend it should not lead us, however, to imagine that the legal interpretation of the 1951 Convention has been static across this period. On the contrary. Recall that Article 2 of the Convention describes refugees as persons who have 'a well-founded fear of being persecuted for reasons of race, religion, nationality, membership of a social group or political opinion'. It is an important feature of the Convention that it leaves the interpretation of this definition to the legal systems of individual states; and this has resulted in a fair degree of variance between states in their interpretations. However, at the same time, the growth of the international human rights regime – especially since the 1970s – has supported important interpretive developments, including an increasing acknowledgement of claims that this definition should be read as encompassing persecution by non-state actors from which the state is not disposed to protect citizens and that threats or conduct amounting to persecution can take gender-specific (and other social identity-specific) forms as well as the form of appeals to the category 'membership of a social group' (encompassing, for example, LGBTI persons).[29] These judicial developments have widened the practical scope of the Convention. But perhaps the most significant development in the area of the interaction between human rights law and the international refugee regime has been the expanded principle of *non-refoulement*, in which the norm of non-refoulement established in the Convention is extended to cover persons who do not fall under the Convention's criteria of refugeehood but have human rights-based grounds not to be returned to their home state. Such 'complementary protection' is 'typically granted where the treatment feared does not reach the level of severity of "persecution", or where there is a risk of persecution but it is not linked to one of the Refugee Convention grounds'.[30] This development has become another site on which the tension between humanitarian and political pictures is played out through a debate on whether non-Convention refugees who are covered by complementary protection should enjoy the same form of domestic legal status as Convention refugees. On the one hand, UNHCR 'has argued that the rights and benefits granted to forced migrants should be based on need rather than the grounds on which they have been granted protection', and

hence 'that there is no valid reason to treat benefi-
ciaries of complementary protection any differently
from Convention refugees'.[31] On the other hand,
scholars such as Durieux and Hathaway express
concern that this erodes the distinctiveness of the
claim of Convention refugees and that 'equal treatment might ultimately dilute the special protection
offered to refugees by the Refugee Convention'.[32]

Conclusion

This all too brief historical reconstruction of the
emergence and development of the international
refugee regime makes visible the sources of, and
the continuing tensions between, humanitarian
and political pictures of refugees. Demonstrating
both the historical roots of these pictures and their
development and interaction in the post-war refugee regime, it accounts for the grip that these two
pictures have on our ethical imaginations. The question it raises for us, caught as we are in the tensions
between the two pictures, is whether it is possible
to makes sense of this history by offering a normative reconstruction of the institution of refugeehood
that transcends their opposition.

2

Who Are Refugees?

In the last chapter we saw how tracing the emergence and development of the modern refugee regime in terms of its core institutions – the Refugee Convention and the UNHCR – have led us to a position in which contemporary refugee protection is characterised by a tension between two depictions of refugees – one *humanitarian*, the other *political* – that play important roles in its formation and subsequent trajectory. The aim of this chapter is to reconstruct the normative basis of the institution of refugeehood in a way that demonstrates the limitations of each of these pictures and moves beyond them. It does so by offering an account of the normative role of the modern refugee regime in relation to the conditions of legitimacy of our global political order and by arguing for the importance of differentiating refugees, conceived of as persons to whom the duty of non-refoulement should apply, in terms of the distinct grounds of their claims and what is communicated by the distinct statuses that granting such claims entails.

Who Is a Refugee?

The aim of providing a coherent normative basis for the contemporary refugee regime, given its expansion beyond the initial terms of the Refugee Convention, is not a new one. In 1985 Andrew Shacknove published the classic article 'Who is a Refugee?' to address this problem. In his article Shacknove acknowledges, as I do, that much of the practical problem of refugee protection results from 'the reluctance of sovereign states to grant political deference and financial support to the relevant international agencies, their hesitancy in assuming the burdens of material relief, asylum, and resettlement, and their concern that assisting refugees could adversely implicate other foreign policy objectives'.[1] We will return to this issue in the final chapter of this book. But Shacknove also makes the important point that 'the problem is only partially attributable to political conflicts and resource scarcity, for conceptual confusion –

about the meaning of refugeehood, its causes, and its management – also contributes to the misery of both refugee and host and to the inflammation of international tension':

> An overly narrow conception of 'refugee' will contribute to the denial of international protection to countless people in dire circumstances whose claim to assistance is impeccable. Ironically, for many persons on the brink of disaster, refugee status is a privileged position. In contrast to other destitute people, the refugee is eligible for many forms of international assistance, including material relief, asylum, and permanent resettlement. Conversely, an overly inclusive conception is also morally suspect and will, in addition, financially exhaust relief programs and impune the credibility of the refugee's privileged position among host populations, whose support is crucial for the viability of international assistance programs.[2]

To this we may add that the presence of both overly narrow and overly broad conceptions within public discourse enables the political exploitation of indeterminacy concerning who is a refugee by governmental and non-governmental actors alike. To address this condition, Shacknove offers a normative reconstruction of the *concept* of refugeehood that justifies the extension of this concept expressed in the 1969 OAU Refugee Convention and further broadens its scope.

The starting point here is the criteria for refugeehood in the 1951 Convention. Shacknove points out that this basic legal concept involves the following assumptions:

(a) A bond of trust, loyalty, protection, and assistance between citizen and state constitutes the normal basis of political society.
(b) In the case of the refugee, this bond has been severed.
(c) Persecution and alienage (being outside one's state) are always the physical manifestations of this severed bond.
(d) These manifestations are necessary and sufficient conditions for determining refugeehood.[3]

But a definition based on these criteria, he argues, is inadequate for the following reasons:

1 Persecution is a sufficient but not necessary condition for the severing of the normal political bond – it is one manifestation of a broader phenomenon: the absence of state protection of citizens' basic needs.

2 Alienage is also not a necessary condition, being one subset of the broader category: the physical access of the international community to the unprotected person.[4]

The argument for (1) is based on the claim that the social compact between state and citizens establishes minimal conditions for the treatment of citizens and of their allegiance to the state and these conditions can be expressed in terms of a set of basic needs – 'physical security, vital subsistence, and liberty of political participation and physical movement' – that are *basic* because they are 'are equally essential for survival'.[5] The argument for (2) is grounded on a distinction within the class of people whose basic needs are unmet by their state in terms of 'their differing positions vis-à-vis the international community', where refugees are distinguished by the fact that they 'have a well-founded fear that recourse to their own government is futile and are, in addition, within reach of the international community'.[6] This last condition is satisfied, on Shacknove's account, *either* if the state requests or allows assistance from the international community *or* if it is unable to prevent such assistance from being provided. Taken together, these arguments lead Shacknove to propose that 'a refugee is, in essence, a person whose government fails to protect his basic needs, who has no remaining recourse than to seek international restitution of these needs, and who is so situated that international assistance is possible'.[7]

Shacknove's analysis thus encompasses and further extends the conception of refugeehood expressed in the 1969 OAU Convention.

It is an important feature of Shacknove's argument that it offers a strategy for attempting to reconcile the humanitarian and the political pictures by linking the humanitarian focus on basic needs to the political focus on membership. It does so through an account of membership in terms of a social compact defined by the provision of basic needs. However, I will argue that, despite its many virtues, Shacknove's attempt to provide a cogent intellectual foundation for the contemporary refugee regime is ultimately unsuccessful and that the roots of its limitations lie in Shacknove's decision to focus on the *concept* of the refugee rather than on the *institution* of refugeehood – that is, on his view that the question of whether state and international agencies have obligations to refugees can be treated as separate from the question of who is a refugee, on the grounds that a 'conception of refugeehood is prior to a theory and policy of entitlements'.[8]

Reflect on the two pictures of refugeehood to which I have drawn attention. In each case, we see linked together a conception of refugees, a ground of obligations to refugees, and a general characterisation of this responsibility and its limits. This is not surprising, because each of these pictures is the expression of a view on *the point and purpose* of the institution of refugeehood, and this is what links and integrates the three elements of conception, ground and responsibility that compose it. The humanitarian picture sees the point and purpose of the international refugee regime in offering relief for the suffering of persons whose state has failed to secure their basic needs and in communicating the commitment of the international order to the moral equality of human beings; the political picture sees it in restoring the political standing of those unjustly denied that standing through persecution and in expressing international condemnation of that denial. These distinct views on the practical role of the international refugee regime find expression in the differences of conception, ground and responsibility between the two pictures. My point is, *contra* Shacknove, that the question 'who is a refugee?' cannot be meaningfully addressed independently of a view about what the point and purpose of the international refugee regime is.

Consider, for example, two alternative views that resist the claims of Shacknove's argument. What we may call the alienage view shares Shacknove's criticism of the necessity of persecution but retains the criterion of alienage in conceptualising refugees as

> those people in need of a new state of residence, either temporarily or permanently, because if forced to return home or remain where they are they would – as a result or either the brutality or inadequacy of their state – be persecuted or seriously jeopardise their physical security or vital subsistence needs.[9]

Those who defend the alienage account argue that

> refugeehood is, in one vital respect, conceptually related to migration; what distinguishes the refugee from other foreigners in need is that he or she is in need of the protection afforded by short or long-term asylum (i.e., residence in a new state) because there is no reasonable prospect of that person finding protection any other way.[10]

This account may be seen, like Shacknove's view, as seeking to reconcile humanitarian and political pictures, but also as making the norm of state sovereignty and non-intervention more central to the functioning of the international refugee regime. Hence it sees a salient difference between international aid to persons inside and outside the state that is registered with the concept and status of 'refugee'. The second alternative is what we may call the surrogate membership view, which offers a direct expression of the political picture. It does so by adopting Rawls's stylised distinction between *outlaw states*, which flout 'the requirements of international legitimacy by violating basic human rights',[11] and *burdened societies*, which are unable to provide adequately for the physical security and basic subsistence needs of their citizens. The point here concerns the distinctiveness of the relationship between asylum and persecution:

> Citizens of burdened societies lack protection of their basic rights, but they retain their standing as members. The appropriate stance of outsiders to burdened societies is to lend assistance, not to condemn their failings. Asylum is an inappropriate tool for addressing the needs of those fleeing burdened societies.[12]

By contrast, this view claims that asylum as a mode of surrogate membership in another state is the appropriate response for dealing with those citizens who are targeted by outlaw states, since it provides these persecuted citizens, whose very standing as members is being denied, with protection 'in a manner that also expresses the condemnation that is deserved'.[13] Central to this alternative and to the criticism it offers is a view of the point and purpose of the international refugee regime as a tool not only for restoring political standing to individuals who are wrongfully denied it but also for acting on outlaw states in ways that are designed to express international commitment to liberal norms and to contribute to altering the conduct of those illiberal states.

Sketching these alternative views, each of which presents a coherent conception of refugees, illustrates the central problem with Shacknove's strategy for seeking to move beyond the opposition between humanitarian and political pictures – and hence also shows what is required in order to do so. What we need is a normative reconstruction of the point and purpose of the institution of refugeehood that makes sense of this institution against the background of the history sketched in the preceding chapter and that can serve to guide our reflection and action with respect to the international refugee regime.

Reconstructing the Institution of Refugeehood

We can begin to approach this task of reconstruction by noting two points about our current global political order. The first is that it is a normative order, oriented both towards the Janus-faced norm of state sovereignty and non-intervention and towards the cosmopolitan norm of human rights. Its claim to legitimacy depends on this dual orientation. This combination finds expression in a division of labour in which securing the human rights of particular persons is primarily to be achieved by way of their allocation to particular states. (Hence the particular importance of protecting individuals from statelessness expressed in the human right to have a nationality.[14]) The second point is that our current global political order is a dispersed regime of global governance[15] in which states are the primary agents through which the regime itself is constituted and reproduced. States are collectively responsible for the character and functioning of this regime of governance; the powers that it grants to states to determine their own nationality laws or to regulate entry at their territorial borders are an example of this situation. States share responsibility because (a) they are co-participants in the practice of governance and recognise one another as co-participants and (b) no participant has the unilateral power to determine the norms of this practice.[16] (This does not mean that they are equally responsible.)

Taking these points together draws our attention to the norm that states have primary responsibility for securing the human rights of their own citizens and to the presumption that states can generally be expected to possess the relevant capabilities and dispositions required to comply with this norm. To the extent that states are not disposed to secure the basic rights of (some of) their citizens or lack the capability to do so, this constructs a legitimacy problem not only for the states in question, but also for the international order of states as a regime of global governance.[17] It does so since it points to the failure of this regime to secure conditions under which states are generally capable of, and disposed to, comply with the norm of basic rights protection whose universal provision underwrites the claim to legitimacy of the international order. The claim to political legitimacy of this regime of global governance hangs on being able to sustain the imagined reconciliation of an international order of sovereign states and a cosmopolitan order of human rights; and the failure of states to secure the basic rights of their citizens threatens the ability of the regime to sustain the minimal conditions of such an imagined reconciliation.

To address the structural problem of states that lack the disposition or the capability (or both) to secure the basic rights of their citizens requires the international community to act on these states, for example through global development programmes and international human rights law, and to develop techniques of global governance that more effectively realise state compliance with the requirements of political legitimacy. However, to address the immediate consequences of state failures to protect basic rights requires *legitimacy repair mechanisms* that not only are compatible with the normative ordering of this dispersed regime of global governance but *act effectively to reaffirm the minimal conditions of the imagined reconciliation of an international order of sovereign states and a cosmopolitan order of human rights*. We can, I submit, see the normative function of the international refugee regime as being such a legitimacy repair mechanism[18] – and indeed as one of two general legitimacy repair mechanisms developed by the regime of global governance, the other being what we might call 'the international emergency assistance regime'. Each of these regimes provides a legitimacy repair mechanism through which a distinct class of those who are subject to non-protecting states can enjoy protection in a way that affirms the dual commitment to state sovereignty and human rights; and this dual commitment is the point and purpose of such regimes.

The difference between them is that, whereas the emergency assistance regime acts as a *supplement* to a functioning state in addressing the basic rights of persons within its territory, the refugee regime acts as a *substitute* for the state in addressing those whose basic rights protection is best served by flight from, or non-return to, the state (or, in cases of a non-functioning state, by constructing international zones of protection). With respect of the refugee regime, Carens puts the general point nicely:

> The modern state system organizes the world so that all of the inhabited land is divided up among (putatively) sovereign states who possess exclusive authority over what goes on within the territories they govern, including the right to control and limit entry to their territories. Almost all human beings are assigned to one, and normally only one, of these states at birth. . . . Even if being assigned to a particular sovereign state works well for most people, it clearly does not work well for refugees. Their state has failed them, either deliberately or through its incapacity. Because the state system assigns people to states, states collectively have a responsibility to help those for whom this assignment is disastrous. The duty to admit refugees can thus be seen as an obligation that emerges from the responsibility to make some provision to correct for the foresee-

able failures of a social institution. Every social institution will generate problems of one sort or another, but one of the responsibilities we have in constructing an institution is to anticipate the ways in which it might fail and to build in solutions for those failures. If people flee from the state of their birth (or citizenship) because it fails to provide them with a place where they can live safely, then other states have a duty to provide a safe haven. Thus, we can see that states have a duty to admit refugees that derives from their own claim to exercise power legitimately in a world divided into states.[19]

We can see a nascent version of this mechanism in the emergence of the figure of the refugee in the Huguenot crisis. The claim to political legitimacy of the regime of European governance required the imagined reconciliation of a European international order of sovereign states with the norms of religious toleration established in the Peace of Westphalia – and the actions of Louis XIV in relation to the Huguenots threatened that claim. Inventing 'the refugee' as a distinct category of migrant and using it to protect those who fled provided a way of repairing the legitimacy problem posed by France's conduct that enacted the reaffirmation of the norms of state sovereignty and religious toleration. Although our contemporary context is different in several respects from that of the Huguenot crisis, we can already discern there the basic form of the refugee as a figure for whom the international order (via a representative state) stands *in loco civitatis*, that is, as a surrogate or substitute for the refugee's state, as taking on responsibilities for which the refugee's state is otherwise accountable.

In its contemporary form and scope, the institution of refugeehood can be understood as one in which refugees are persons whose basic rights are unprotected by their state and can only be protected through recourse to the international order of states acting *in loco civitatis* and thereby affirming the dual commitment of the regime of global governance to the norms of state sovereignty and human rights. Notably this view of the scope of the institution of refugeehood differs from both Shacknove's basic needs conception and the alienage account – and does so precisely because it expresses the dual commitment to state sovereignty and human rights.

Imagine two different types of scenario. In the first, a burdened society is incapable of securing basic rights for its citizens in the face of, say, famine or environment degradation and calls for international assistance. In the second, the basic rights of the citizens of a burdened society are violated because the domestic governmental order has entirely broken down under conditions of, say, civil war and the international community has constructed 'safe havens' within the borders of the state to protect non-combatant citizens. Both of these scenarios would fit the basic needs account's criteria for granting refugeehood, whereas on the alienage account citizens who remain within the borders of their state would not be entitled to refugeehood in either scenario. On the legitimacy view proposed here, however, there is a salient difference between the two scenarios that is not picked up by either of these accounts. The first type of case is one in which the 'home' state is acting effectively to secure its citizens' basic rights precisely by calling for international assistance in order to supplement its capabilities, and aims to build these capabilities with such international assistance. The second type of case is one in which the international community is required to act as a surrogate for the state in order to secure the basic rights of those threatened. In the former, the international community *supplements* the state; in the latter, the international community *substitutes* for the state.

This difference accounts for the centrality of the norm of non-refoulement to the institution of refugeehood. In the cases envisaged by the basic needs view, where the international community supplements the state, this norm would be redundant. Acknowledging the centrality of non-refoulement might then lead us to endorse the alienage view. However, we should note that, in cases where the government of a state has broken down so completely that there is no agent that can reasonably claim to serve as the political representative of the state (examples from recent history would include the governmental collapse in Somalia and the break-up of the former Yugoslavia), agents of the international community can legitimately enter and establish safe havens as de facto international territories within the territory of this nominal state. In such circumstances the norm of non-refoulement still applies, but has the specific and special sense of not returning persons from safe havens to territory within the state that falls outside such international territorial zones.[20] In distinguishing between these two types of cases, the legitimacy-based *in loco civitatis* view makes better normative sense of the centrality of the norm of non-refoulement (and of its development beyond Convention refugees) to the institution of refugeehood – and of how this norm enacts the affirmation of the global political order's dual commitment to state sovereignty and to basic human rights.

However, by specifying the scope of the institution of refugeehood in this manner, this account may seem to expose itself to objections from those committed to the political picture of refugees – namely that, in encompassing the different kinds of cases that fall under UNHCR practice, the account fails to register (1) the distinctiveness of refugees as persons subject to the threat of persecution and (2) the expressive role of the granting of asylum as a communicative act that condemns the persecuting state. Notice, however, that this second objection derives its force from the unstated assumption that refugeehood is, and must be, a single undifferentiated category to which asylum is the sole response. But there is no compelling reason to adopt such an assumption and, as we have seen, the historical practice of refugee protection offers a more complex picture than this objection admits. Viewed in this light, the character of this objection is better conceived of as drawing attention to the point that the complexities of refugee protection practice are not currently well signalled by distinct legal statuses that differentiate types of refugees in terms of the diverse relationships that standing *in loco civitatis* may involve. Within the general class of refugees as persons who fall under the principle of non-refoulement, we have good reasons to establish distinct legal statuses that differentiate between types of refugees according to the distinct grounds of their claims and the expressive roles of granting appropriate forms of protection to them. The general concept of standing *in loco civitatis* (like that of standing *in loco parentis*) not only is compatible with differentiating between cases that call for distinct treatment but, I will argue, requires such differentiation, if the institution of refugeehood is to play its legitimacy repair role effectively. In the remainder of this chapter I develop this case by describing three normative statuses – asylum, sanctuary and refuge – that, I propose, should be differentiated, along with what is owed to each of these types of refugee. Here I lay out the basic scheme of differentiation and in the next chapter I elaborate in greater depth on responsibilities owed to each type of refugee.

Asylum

Being persecuted for one's religious or political beliefs, or because one is a member of an ethnic or social group, is a distinctive wrong and also a serious harm. Today the Rohingya from Myanmar serve as one clear example of such persecution; another is provided by the LGBTI refugees in flight from any of the 77 states in which their identity is criminalised (or any of the many other states in which the state is not disposed to protect them from persecuting non-state agents). The wrong consists in the rights-breaching denial of one's equal standing as a member of the state and, hence, in an international order of states of one's equal standing as a member of global political society. The harm consists in the fact that, by being rendered de facto stateless, one is made acutely vulnerable both to contingencies of circumstance and to the agency of public or private others. Here we can endorse Price's view that a grant of asylum can be seen as expressing condemnation of the persecuting state (or of the state that is not disposed to protect from persecution)[21] and Cherem's defence of the specificity of persecution, as well as the view expressed by both these authors that central to asylum is the granting of a claim to membership. Price argues that such refugees are people who

> not only face a threat to their bodily integrity or liberty; they are also effectively expelled from their political communities. They are not only victims, but also exiles. Asylum responds not only to victims' need for protection, but also to their need for political standing, by extending membership in a new political community.[22]

This argument does not depend on whether the persons entitled to asylum will immediately identify politically with the state of new member-ship,[23] or on whether they may later choose to return to their state of original nationality under transformed conditions, but on the obligation to assert, through the granting of new membership, the political standing of persons who have been wrongfully denied it by their home state. In a world in which state membership is the basic condition of political standing, it is a duty of the international order of states to ensure that all persons enjoy such standing and, when it is wrongfully denied through persecution,[24] to provide protection in a way that reaffirms the right to it. This is what the legal status of asylum as a distinctive type of refugee status should be conceived of as providing. Hence a person who reaches a border and advances a claim to asylum is asserting a claim against that state (as a representative of the international order of states) that not only entitles this person to a fair process of determination but, supposing the claim is validated, makes that state responsible for ensuring that this person is not returned to the home state but is granted new membership in a state (which may or may not be the state of asylum determination) where there are good reasons to be confident that this person's security, liberty and welfare will be protected.

Sanctuary

Whereas asylum is an appropriate response to persons who are (or have good reason to believe that they will be) *targeted* for persecution by their state of nationality or *identified* by it as persons whom this state is not disposed to protect from persecution by private agents (each of which wrongfully denies the standing of such persons as members), it does not align well with the claims of persons who are fleeing generalised violence and the breakdown of public order – persons who are not targets but rather would fall into the condition of being, as it were, collateral damage – or with the claims of persons whom the state is incapable of protecting from persecution by non-state agents. Many of those fleeing the civil war in Syria may fall into this category, as would many refugees encamped in African states such as Kenya and Uganda. The extension of the 1951 Convention definition in the 1969 OAU Convention is an acknowledgement of the claim of such persons to protection, which, given the norm of non-intervention, will generally require that they have crossed an international border (unless the safe havens scenario applies).

The claim advanced against the states to which such persons flee (or against the relevant international agents, in the case of safe havens) as representatives of the international community is a claim to *sanctuary*, conceived of as a space where one is protected against the threats to one's basic security, liberty and welfare posed by generalised violence and the breakdown of public order in one's home state (or, in the absence of generalised conditions, by the incapacity of the state to protect one from private agents), without fear of being returned to that state as long as the relevant conditions persist. Notice that the relationship to membership is rather different in this case from what it is in cases of claim to asylum. It is not that one's political standing has been wrongfully denied and needs to be reasserted, but rather that it has become harmfully ineffective – or, perhaps better, inoperative, in the sense that it does not play the protective or enabling roles *within* the relevant state that define its effective functioning. (This inoperative citizenship is not formally identical to the de facto statelessness of the asylum refugee, although it may still amount to a condition equivalent to de facto statelessness.) In this context, the primary responsibility of the state that adjudicates the status of sanctuary seekers is to ensure that, if their claims are valid, they are subject to the norm of non-refoulement and have access to the basic security, liberty and welfare that the protective and enabling functions of citizenship would normally provide. This does not *require* rapid admission to a new membership, although the refugee's absence of an effective citizenship should encourage such a process, nor does it automatically rule out non-voluntary repatriation in the way in which asylum should be understood as entailing.[25] Rather the relationship to membership is an altogether more temporally complex issue in contexts of sanctuary, where at least three considerations are in play.

The first is that to be a person requiring sanctuary

is not simply to be an individual who has lost the protection of her basic rights; it is to be someone deprived of her social world. It is to be someone who has been displaced from the communities, associations, relationships and cultural context that have shaped one's identity and around which one's life plan has hitherto been organised. Unsurprisingly, then, refugees often describe their experience as one of confusion, dispossession, and disempowerment. As one Somali refugee who sought asylum in Italy described his experience: 'there's a total void, a feeling of total disorientation'.[26]

The second consideration is that it is a pervasive feature of refugee crises that their time horizon is liable to be indeterminate – which explains the consequent positioning of refugees as persons who are situated in a condition of social and civic limbo, unable to commit to building a new life because they may be returned to the old, unable to commit to the old life because they may never be able to take it up once more.[27] To be a person requiring sanctuary is, to a very significant degree, to lack an ability that is taken for granted by citizens who conduct their lives against the background of a right to secure residence in a state, namely the ability to plan their future, to make choices about the medium-term or long-term direction of their lives. Everyday social contexts shape the horizon within which persons coherently conceive of, and act to realise, their future selves – and to inhabit a condition in which the social conditions of one's agency are constitutively open to being ruptured through repatriation is to lack a secure horizon in which to engage in the activity of planning and shaping one's future.

The third consideration pertains to the states that offer sanctuary and to their citizens, for whom providing the basic security, liberty and welfare that the protective and enabling functions of citizenship would normally offer and providing citizenship are distinct commitments. The question raised by this consideration concerns whether and when states of sanctuary acquire a duty to enable persons of sanctuary to acquire membership of the protective state (and hence become legally immune from non-voluntary repatriation). It may be supposed that such persons should, at the very least, enjoy the same conditions of access to membership as those owed to lawfully resident migrants in general (excluding any requirements to surrender their existing nationality); and, given the distinctive challenge of their circumstances, namely that they lack effective citizenship, there are strong grounds to think that more rapid access to membership would be not only justified but also called for.[28] That persons of sanctuary are not a matter of 'voluntary admissions' on the part of the state does not undermine this claim; rather it highlights the point that considerations of fairness to states of sanctuary count when it comes to the division of international responsibility sharing for such persons, precisely because granting sanctuary entails duties to admit to membership after a reasonable period of residence.[29]

Refuge

The distinctiveness of the case of refuge is that it applies in the context of discrete and specific events such as a famine or natural disaster,[30] where a person is so situated that she can save herself from the threat to her basic rights posed by the event in question by seeking immediate shelter across an international border and that this is her best reasonable option in the circumstances in which she finds herself. Grants of refuge thus act to acknowledge and express a commitment to the basic rights of persons in the face of circumstances beyond the immediate control of their home state, and repatriation as soon as reasonable is the appropriate response. Refuge here serves the same basic function as international emergency assistance to persons displaced by the relevant events within the state, and is essentially part of the same emergency assistance policy toolkit. It generates no basis for claims of membership in the state of refuge or, typically, of social integration in that state, unless the refugee's displacement becomes protracted. The role of non-refoulement in relation to the status of refuge is to secure persons against being returned to circumstances where, through no fault of their home state, their basic rights cannot be protected.

*

Distinguishing three types of claim to refugee status in the separate legal statuses of asylum, sanctuary and refuge is not only appropriately responsive to the relevant person's distinct grounds for flight (and hence discloses the distinct relations to persons that standing *in loco civitatis* can require), but also essential to the proper functioning of the institution of refugeehood within global political society in its communicative role. Each type of status signals a distinct requirement made to the international community – distinct in terms of action not only towards refugees but also towards the state from which they flee (or to which they are unwilling to return).

Under the former aspect, each status picks out distinct criteria that are relevant to the international division of responsibility for refugee protection. The status of *asylum* makes civic standing and integration central in ways that render salient both the refugee's choice of a state of asylum and human rights security, as key criteria for dividing responsibility. The status of *sanctuary* positions social integration as pivotal and may be taken as identifying support for refugee dignity and self-reliance through educational, employment and welfare provision, and support for cultural community as key elements for fair division of responsibility. The status of *refuge* identifies access to immediate emergency assistance as the key criterion.

Under the latter aspect, each status communicates judgments by protecting states concerning the appropriate mode of response on the part of the international community to the state from which refugees flee. The status of *asylum* expresses condemnation of (unwillingness to protect from) persecution exercised by the home state, and hence the duty of the international community to act (in legitimate ways) on that state in order to try to bring it into conformity with the appropriate dispositional norm. This may involve sanctions of various kinds. The status of *sanctuary* expresses political concern about the breakdown of public order in the home state, and hence the duty of the international community to support the reestablishment of public order there. This may call for peace-building efforts, for example. The status of *refuge* expresses international concern about the circumstances confronted by the home state, and hence the duty of the international community to provide emergency assistance. If the international refugee regime is to be a well-functioning regime, it is important not only that it provides the appropriate support to the distinct types of refugee but also that it communicates the appropriate requirements of international response to the home state in terms of the specific legitimacy issues raised by each type of flight.

Such an internal differentiation of refugeehood avoids the radical narrowing of the application of the norm of non-refoulement represented by Price's and Cherem's 'political' views, which abstract from the practice of the modern refugee regime; but it also avoids the flattening of distinctions and the failure of appropriate communicative clarity represented by the 'humanitarian' picture.[31] It thus provides a normative reconstruction of the institution of refugeehood that is capable of encompassing the modern practice of refugee protection but supports better the legitimacy repair work that the institution serves. The implication of this view for refugee protection will be further developed over the next two chapters.

3

Responsibility for Refugees

Shared Responsibilities and Durable Solutions

If we consider refugee protection from the point of view of the UNHCR, then we think of this kind of protection as an *ethics of rescue* in which the responsibility to help is predicated on the capacity to help without incurring undue costs, as in the case of the child drowning in the pond. Refugee protection is, on this view, a matter of *remedial responsibility*, to be divided between agents of protection according to their relative capacities to help; and the provenance of the refugee flow (or, by analogy, how the child came to be drowning in the pond) is not taken to be directly relevant to the distribution of the responsibility to rescue. What counts is the immediate need and the relative capacity of agents to address it. By contrast, on the reconstruction of the institution of refugeehood advanced in the last chapter, refugee protection is best construed as a matter of *redressing the wrongs and harms to which refugees are subject*. It is an issue of reparation (whether in the form of restitution, compensation, or satisfaction) for the failure of the international order of states to secure the conditions under which individuals and groups can enjoy basic rights in their own states. On this view, as we'll see, the provenance of refugee flows does matter to the fair allocation of responsibility.[1]

In the present chapter the focus turns to the implications that this reconstruction of refugeehood has on the matter of *who* owes *what* to refugees. I have already touched on the question of what is owed in the form of responsibilities by characterising the general status of refugeehood through the norm of non-refoulement and by differentiating between refugees according to the three types of asylum, sanctuary and refuge. This chapter begins by elaborating on the implications of non-refoulement for responsibility, then turns to the relationships of asylum, sanctuary and refuge with the three main forms of durable solution that are salient to refugee protection: repatriation, local integration, third-country resettlement. Having clarified the responsibilities owed to refugees, I turn to the critical question of how these responsibilities should be shared among the states that make up the international order, then to the relationship between the sharing of responsibility and the provenance of refugees flows.

The Responsibility to Protect and the Norm of Non-Refoulement

The norm of non-refoulement is the distinguishing feature of the general status of refugeehood. It places the state into which an individual seeking refugee status crosses under a strict duty not to return that person to any territory where her basic rights are at risk. This duty persists as long as the individual remains entitled to that status. This does not entail that refugees have a right to asylum, sanctuary or refuge in the state to which they make application; states may come to any of a range of reasonable agreements with each other concerning how best to protect refugees, including ones in which the state that processes the claim to refugeehood is not that which provides, for example, asylum. The duty of non-refoulement thus establishes a general default condition, which is binding on all states in which the minimum requirement of the general responsibility for refugee protection – not to return someone to a place where that person's basic rights are threatened – takes priority over the fair sharing of that general responsibility among states.

This is as it should be. To see why, imagine a world in which states know what their fair shares of refugee protection would be under the assumption that every state does its fair share. Suppose that some states do what would count as their fair share under these conditions, while others don't. Could those states that have done what would count as their fair share under conditions of full compliance legitimately claim that they have done all that is required of them and that they are thereby justified in engaging in direct or indirect refoulement with any further refugees? Hardly. The reason why such a claim would not be legitimate is that the general responsibility to provide refugee protection is a collective responsibility of the international order of states, and *the responsibility for securing compliance is part of this general responsibility.* For a state to refuse to comply with the norm of non-refoulement on the grounds that it has done what would be its fair share under conditions of full compliance when such conditions do not obtain is to shift illegitimately the costs of the failure to secure full compliance from the group that owes the general obligation on to the group to which it is owed—to offload the costs of the failure from states on to refugees.[2]

In establishing this default condition, the norm of non-refoulement thus represents the legitimate priority accorded to securing the minimum requirement of refugee protection over the fair sharing of the general responsibility for refugee protection. But notice that, in doing so, it establishes *only* a binding minimum requirement and leaves it open to states to work out reasonable terms of cooperation for determining how full reparative responsibility for refugees is to be best achieved. In this way, the norm of non-refoulement mediates between the norms of state sovereignty and human rights in a way that expresses the dual commitment to both norms to the fullest extent compatible with ensuring the legitimacy-repair role of the institution of refugeehood.

Refugee Statuses and Durable Solutions

Let me now turn to considering reparative responsibilities to refugees that extend beyond the minimum established by the norm of non-refoulement. I will do this by returning to the three refugee statuses distinguished in the previous chapter in relation to the three types of durable solution – repatriation, local integration, and resettlement – prevalent in the international refugee regime.

Asylum

Central to the grant of asylum is the acknowledgement that a refugee is subject to the threat of persecution in his home state, and thus that his standing as a member of the political community is wrongfully denied. Asylum refugees are wrongfully made de facto stateless; hence the relevant form of reparation is to provide, first, surrogate membership and, second, reasonably rapid access to membership of a new state. We may think of this reparative action as the relevant form of *restitution* to asylum refugees. The status of asylum thus aligns directly with either *settlement* in the asylum-granting state or *resettlement*, which is a process of transfer from the state in which refugeehood is recognised to the state in which new membership is acquired. Settlement is appropriate where this manner of proceeding supports the fair distribution of responsibility for the appropriate protection of refugees and hence should be the default assumption in asylum claims made on states of the global North. On the same basis, resettlement from the state of initial recognition and immediate safety should be the preferred policy for asylum claims advanced in states of the global South. This argument from fairness is further supported by the specific salience of a condition of robust rights protection in the state of new membership for persons who have been persecuted and stripped of their political standing in their home state; and such rights security may not be robustly available in southern states of recognition. Moreover, the state of immediate safety is typically a state that neighbours the home state from which the person seeking asylum has fled; and, while in contexts of sanctuary and refuge this may be an advantage, it is unlikely to be so in cases where actual or threatened persecution is involved, given the reasonable fear that one is still within relatively easy reach of the persecuting agents.

We should note two corollaries of the argument thus far. The first is that, in the absence of fair, efficient and effective resettlement processes, refugees have no obligation to enter their claim to asylum in the state of immediate safety or, indeed, in any state that does not clearly and obviously meet the relevant standards of rights security. The second is that states that can offer the relevant level of robust rights security can be reasonably seen as having an obligation to privilege the responsibility to address the protection of asylum refugees through direct admission or through resettlement within their share of the general responsibility for refugee protection. This is not to justify the distinction between host states (Kenya, Lebanon, Jordan) that generally do not grant asylum in the sense of giving refugees a permanent status (though they allow them to reside indefinitely) and asylum-granting states such as the United States or Germany, which offer asylum in the sense of a permanent status with a path to citizenship, but to recognise what this distinction points to within the overall scheme of refugee protection, namely the need for states of the global North with robust rights protections to play a central role in the protection of asylum refugees until such protections are more widely available. *It is notable that the current provision of resettlement places by these states offers only a small fraction of what is required.*

The default assumption of a grant of asylum—that the refugee will become a permanent member of a new state—also has significance for the role that the refugee's own reasons for wanting membership in one state rather than another should play in this process. Consider that, in general, it is desirable that citizens of a state (which meets at least the minimal legitimacy threshold) identify the conditions of their own autonomy and well-being with the conditions of autonomy and well-being of their political community. This identification underwrites civic solidarity, and we may think of the cultivation of this identification as a process of civic integration.[3] This being so, factors that predispose a refugee to identify with a state of new membership (e.g. existing family relationships, or an established home state diaspora in that state, fluency in the language, particularly salient opportunities for educational or professional development, etc.) should carry weight in the process of determining where they are resettled. These factors and the way particular refugees weight them may be very heterogeneous; some factors (e.g. family relations) may pick out a particular state, others (e.g. language) may be satisfiable by several states. The important point is that such reasons matter for the purposes served by the grant of asylum and should be given due weight in any reasonable scheme of international cooperation for protecting asylum refugees.

Finally, we should not neglect the question of what the home state of the refugee owes both to the states that provide immediate safety, asylum, and membership and to the refugee. Here it may be helpful to distinguish (a) the case of 'the persecuting state', which owes compensation to the states that incur costs in having to assume the protective and enabling functions that the home state owed to its refugee-citizen, from (b) the case of 'the no longer persecuting state', which owes reparation to its refugee-citizen. With respect to the persecuting state, my point is that, if appropriate mechanisms are available or can be developed, it would not be unreasonable for the international order of states to establish a system of penalties in order to compensate the protecting states for the work of refugee protection that they assume, insofar as this is part of their share of the general responsibility of refugee protection. With regard to the state that no longer persecutes, each of the three main forms of reparation – restitution, compensation, and satisfaction – comes into play. First, it is important that the state acknowledges its wrongdoing to the asylum refugee; this is the basic form that reparation-as-satisfaction takes. Second, this state has a presumptive obligation to compensate the asylum refugee for the harms endured as a product of its wrongdoing. Third, the state owes a presumptive duty of restitution in the form of affirming the entitlement of the asylum refugee to full standing as a member of her political community. The asylum refugee, who is (on the path to being) a member of a new state, may or may not wish to avail herself of this offer – and neither the fact of the offer nor her choice in this matter should have any consequences for the (acquisition of) membership in the new state. Rather the potential for dual nationality – and hence for freedom of movement between the two states of nationality – should be regarded as providing restitution in a form that acknowledges the personal membership history of the refugee and the particular importance of her interest in robust rights security, given that history.

Sanctuary

The grant of sanctuary acknowledges the responsibility of the international community to persons whose citizenship has not been denied but has become ineffective or inoperative as a result of the breakdown of public order in their home state. This status stands in a more complex relationship to the durable solutions of repatriation, local integration and resettlement, since this complex relationship depends significantly on the ability of the international community effectively to support the restoration of public order in the home state, on the time frame within which it occurs, and on the sources of the breakdown of public order.

The loss of effective citizenship experienced by those who have fled conditions of generalised violence or a breakdown of public order can be conceived of as a loss of the reasonable conditions of effective social agency, for which operative citizenship plays protective and enabling functions. To this experience of social powerlessness in the home state is then added the experience of social disorientation, which comes with arrival in the unfamiliar social environment of another state. To repair this situation means providing sanctuary refugees with conditions under which they can reasonably experience themselves as effective social agents, as agents who can make choices and plans about their future that are not simply driven by the urgent requirements of practical necessity and who have some ability to shape the social environment in which those choices and plans are made.

It may reasonably be pointed out that disorientation is likely to be less stark in states that share significant cultural features with the home state of the refugee; and it may be significantly mitigated in states that have an established diasporic community from that home state (as in the case of preexisting Syrian diasporas in Europe).[4] This is relevant to the question of which states are best placed to support sanctuary refugees; but so too is the capacity of a state for providing reasonable conditions of effective social agency. The basic requirements of this reparative responsibility could be expressed as provision of access to housing, health and welfare systems designed to protect sanctuary refugees from the overwhelming demands of practical necessity; provision of access to opportunities for education, training or employment that should enable sanctuary refugees to make effective choices and plans about their lives; and provision of access to municipal political membership, in order to enable sanctuary refugees to experience themselves as having some say over the environment in which they are situated. Each of these provisions are routes of social integration for refugees within the state of sanctuary; but the second and third are particularly important, as they involve the active participation of refugees in the social and political community of the locality where they are situated. A reparative scheme that denied sanctuary refugees the opportunity for participation in education or employment and for local political participation would not only severely limit the ability of refugees to experience themselves as effective social agents, it would also be liable to propagate, among citizens of the sanctuary state, a demeaning picture of refugees as passive victims and civic burdens, entities who are not 'real people' anymore – *and this is all too often the condition that refugees face today, approximately half of refugees being in urban and peri-urban settings and only a small fraction of these receiving support.* Thus

the ability to provide these kinds of basic requirements of social integration will also be an important
consideration for the sharing of responsibility for
sanctuary among states (where such sharing may
take the form of some states acting as sites of sanctuary and others acting as supporters of sanctuary
by providing skills and resources, for example).

These reflections may seem to lead fairly natu-
rally to the alignment of sanctuary with the durable
solution of local integration in contexts in which
sanctuary refugees are likely to pass the temporal
threshold that should entitle them to membership
of the state of sanctuary. It is important to note,
however, that preventing some states (typically,
proximate states of immediate safety) from having
to bear an unreasonable share of responsibility for
refugee protection is likely to require a scheme of
international cooperation that provides both fair
sharing of responsibility for sanctuary refugees and
safe transit from states of immediate safety to states
of sanctuary. Here the use of mechanisms of allocation that 'match' the legitimate and considered
preferences of refugees and of states and thereby
allows all parties to see their choices as having
shaped their relationship may play a valuable role,[5]
alongside attention to securing appropriate protection for specific vulnerabilities that are differentially

distributed among the refugee population (disability, young children, etc.)

At this stage, however, we should recall that in the previous chapter I argued that sanctuary refugeehood, in contrast to asylum, does not automatically rule out non-voluntary repatriation. This may not appear to sit easily with the preceding focus on local integration. However, the appearance of conflict is significantly reduced when we consider the constraints on legitimate non-voluntary repatriation in sanctuary contexts. The first is that the possibility of non-voluntary repatriation must be subject to strict temporal limits. Sanctuary refugees should be entitled to at least the same fair opportunities for naturalisation in the state of residence as apply to 'voluntary' migrants. After a certain period of time, lawful residents of a society should be considered full members of that society and thereby entitled to political membership.[6] The second constraint is that conditions in the home state of sanctuary refugees must not only have seen the restoration of public order but also be capable of supporting the reintegration of refugees, under conditions in which they possess effective citizenship in that state.[7] The third is that the act of involuntary repatriation should not unreasonably disadvantage or harm sanctuary refugees subject to this process. Thus, for example, involuntary repatriation in the case of a refugee who arrived in the state of sanctuary as a child (either unaccompanied or with parents who have since died) and thereby has only a weak connection to the home state, having lived the critical parts of her life and having her core social relationships in the state of sanctuary, would be unreasonable. The same would be true of a refugee who has formed a personal partnership with a member of the state of sanctuary, or of one who, subject to fair compensation by the sanctuary state, has established a business or career that he would be unable effectively to maintain if involuntarily returned to his home state. Nor is harm to the sanctuary refugee the only consideration. Local communities may also advance reasons that rule out the involuntary repatriation of refugees on the basis of the harm that this would do to the community. The presumptive entitlement of the state of sanctuary to engage in non-voluntary repatriation is thus highly conditional and may be defeated on various grounds.

The fact that the conditions governing legitimate non-voluntary repatriation are demanding has a further important implication, namely that this kind of action draws attention to the fact that states may be subject to political incentives to abuse the power of involuntary repatriation and, insofar as they have the discretion to judge when the conditions for it are met, have the potential to do so. The current policy of involuntary return of refugees to Afghanistan practised by a number of European states is a clear example of such abuse.[8] In the absence of the ability to impose strict checks on the use of this power to return, considerations of fairness and prudence would support restricting it to *voluntary* repatriation, where sanctuary refugees are concerned.

There is no doubt that, under appropriate conditions, voluntary repatriation can play a role alongside local integration in offering a durable solution for sanctuary refugees. It is worth noting, though, that, while local integration leading eventually to membership and voluntary repatriation are often framed as mutually exclusive, there is no need to regard them as such. Indeed, sanctuary refugees who have acquired membership of the state of sanctuary and thereby become dual nationals may reasonably feel more secure in exercising the choice to return to their state of origin, given that they retain, as naturalised citizens, the right to re-enter the state of sanctuary at any time, while their connections to the state of sanctuary also provide a resource for building stronger links between the two states (in terms of economic, cultural or social relationships) to the benefit of each. Furthermore, in the likely event that some sanctuary refugees choose to return while other choose to stay, the resulting transnational relationship between home state citizens and the sanctuary state diaspora can, given supportive policies in these states, similarly serve as a resource that works to the developmental advantage of both states.

What of the obligations of the home state? Much here will be highly contextual and in part dependent on the provenance of and responsibility for the refugee-producing events, but two general responsibilities clearly apply in a post-conflict context. The first is working – with international assistance, where required – to establish the general conditions of just return that enable sanctuary refugees to enjoy the option of return as a real rather than notional option. The second is engaging in a general process of reparations – supported by the international community, as required – to all affected citizens, wherever they reside, that at the very least offers satisfaction by acknowledging the wrongs and harms endured during the period in which the state was unable to protect the basic rights of (some of) its citizens. This might take the form of a 'truth and reconciliation' process, for example; but it might also involve such features as allowing dual nationality to those who have acquired the nationality of the state of sanctuary, establishing expatriate voting rights for those who choose not to return, and adopting a range of diaspora engagement policies where there is reason to think that these types of policy can strengthen the capacity and disposition for basic rights protection in the home state.

Refuge

The case of (presumptively) temporary refuge is different in that it represents the point of overlap of the international refugee regime and the international emergency assistance regime. Persons entitled to refuge are owed temporary protection of their basic rights in the state of refuge but, as long as this condition does not persist long enough to trigger social membership constraints, can be subject to involuntary return as soon as the relevant protection of their basic rights is available to them in their home state (even if this protection is not in the specific area in which they reside). In contrast to sanctuary, refuge is explicitly intended as a temporary status, which does not generate the same incentives for abuse; hence the power of involuntary return exercised by the state of refuge requires only international oversight. Whereas asylum refugees and sanctuary refugees have no obligation to apply for refuge status in the first state of immediate safety where they arrive, claimants of refuge can be taken to be so obliged, since the need for immediate safety is the ground for their claim to protection. Moreover, as the point of overlap of the international refugee regime and the international assistance regime, provision of protection for persons of refuge status is compatible with, and typically served by, a division of labour between proximate states, which have the responsibility of serving as sites of refuge, and the wider international community, whose responsibility it is to provide the skills and resources for the additional assistance requirements of temporary protection. It is important to stress, though, both that the camps in which refuge refugees seek protection need to provide genuine security and that encampment should be a temporary condition.[9]

*

This discussion of responsibility and durable solutions in relation to the distinct types of refugees makes two important points for my overall concerns. The first is that the differences that have emerged reinforce the importance of making such distinctions of status if the refugee regime is to respond appropriately to the grounds on which claims to refugeehood can be legitimately advanced.

The second is that, with respect to the sharing of the general responsibility for refugee protection, this discussion already points to some salient differences between states that are relevant to delivering such protection effectively (robust rights security for asylum, capacities for cultural and social integration for sanctuary, proximity for refuge) and between the roles that refugee (and state) choices should play in the discharge of this responsibility. But in order to develop this argument further I need to turn to offering an account of the more general criteria that should govern the responsibilities owed by particular states within which the considerations offered thus far can be situated.

Sharing Responsibility

Let us begin with two distinctions. The first distinction is between general responsibility and special responsibility. This distinction registers the following point: the fact that the international order of states has a general responsibility to refugees does not entail that specific states may not have special responsibilities to specific refugees in virtue of their unjust acts (or omissions) foreseeably contributing to the production of these refugees.

Consider the following examples relating to the three types of refugee status:

ASYLUM   State A actively supports a dictatorial regime in state B, with the reasonably foreseeable consequence that particular individuals or groups are liable to be subject to persecution by state B (or by non-state actors from which the state is not disposed to protect them).

SANCTUARY   States A, B and C illegitimately act to produce, enable or exacerbate the breakdown of public order and the spread of generalised violence in state D, with the reasonably foreseeable consequence that affected citizens of state D have compelling reason either to flee its territory or not to return to it.

REFUGE   State A has a clearly identifiable remedial responsibility to aid state B, which is suffering from a famine and does not discharge its responsibility appropriately, with the foreseeable consequence that some citizens of state B are driven to leave its territory.

In each of these cases there are specific external states that bear some significant portion of outcome responsibility for a given refugee flow, because the unjust actions (or omissions) of these states *directly and foreseeably* contributed to the production of that flow – and this grounds a special obligation on their part towards the refugees involved.[10]

The second distinction is between general responsibility and particular responsibility. Consider, for example, a case in which Ahmed and his family are refugees seeking sanctuary. Given the intrinsic value of family life and the special importance of family reunification in refugee contexts, the state that grants sanctuary to Ahmed by way of a discharge of its general responsibility to refugees thereby acquires a particular responsibility for granting sanctuary to Ahmed's wife, Fatima, and to his children, Mohammed and Nur.

The important point of difference between special responsibilities and particular responsibilities is that discharging the latter counts as part of the state's fulfilment of its share of general responsibility for refugee protection, whereas discharging the former does not. To see why, consider an analogy. Alf, Bert, Charlie and Dick hire the village hall to have a party. They all have a general responsibility to share fairly the costs of hiring the hall and the burdens of cleaning it up after the party so as to restore the hall to something equivalent to its pre-party condition. However, Dick turns up already drunk and carelessly breaks a window. In these circumstances, it would be unreasonable to expect Alf,

Bert and Charlie to share the costs of hiring a glazier to repair the window – or, to put the same point
the other way around, Dick could not reasonably
argue that his payment to the glazier should count
towards his share of the general responsibility to
restore the hall to something like its pre-party condition. Special obligations should then be treated
separately from the sharing of general responsibility
for refugee protection, that is, for the protection
of refugees whose situation is best seen as an event
for which no particular external state (or group of
states) is foreseeably responsible. But what criteria
should govern the sharing of general responsibility?

All states have a general responsibility to support the conditions of political legitimacy of the
international order of states – and hence to support
global governance practices that develop the capacity and disposition of states to secure the basic
rights of their citizens, and thereby to sustain the
dual commitment to state sovereignty and human
rights. An international order of states in which
some states are unable or unwilling to protect the
basic rights of (some of) their citizens is an unjust
condition; and the responsibility for addressing this
condition lies with the international order of states.
From this standpoint we can plausibly identify two
salient criteria that are relevant to the division of

responsibility. The first is the degree to which a state *contributes* to sustaining this unjust condition by failing to do its fair share of supporting the universal securing of basic rights – where 'fair share' is a matter of the state's relative capacity to contribute to this goal. The second criterion is the degree to which a state *benefits* from the unjust condition – where 'benefit' is expressed in the comparative advantage enjoyed by citizens as a result of this condition. The share of general responsibility owed by a state will, at least in part, be a function of its relative contribution to and relative benefit from the conditions of background injustice that make the generation of refugees a prevalent feature of our global political life. In practice, this means that, in general, the wealthy, 'rule-making' states of the global North bear greater responsibilities than the poorer, 'rule-taking' states of the global South.

But, alongside contribution and benefit, we also need to consider states' relative capacities to protect refugees. Giving protection to refugees is not a cost-free activity for the citizens of the protecting states, and the relative capacities of states to offer refugee protection at a given level of cost per capita that is incurred by their citizens will vary. Recall, however, that the matter of what capacities are relevant also varies across the different types of refugee protection, so that a state's relative capacity for protection of asylum refugees may be quite different from its relative capacity for protection of sanctuary refugees or persons of refuge. Moreover, what a state's relative capacity for a given form of refugee protection is may further vary depending on the scheme of cooperation between states. For example, imagine two states situated in the proximity of a third, which suffers from a civil war; in the circumstances, each of the two acquires a significant number of people who are seeking sanctuary. State A is wealthy but very densely populated. State B is poor and has a low population density. In a scheme in which each state is expected to bear the full costs of providing sanctuary, the relative capacity of each will be limited (by population density for A, by poverty for B), whereas in a scheme in which each contributes on the basis of their joint capacities (e.g. A provides most of the funds, B provides most of the land), the relative capacity of each is significantly increased, and so is the overall capacity for providing sanctuary, too (at a given level of cost). A state's relative capacity is thus conditional both on the types of refugee protection in which it is engaged and on the overall scheme of refugee protection. This is not to support any particular scheme but merely to note that 'capacity' is not something given independently of these considerations.

Towards a Fair Regime of Refugee Protection

The arguments of the preceding sections should lead us to acknowledge the ethical complexity of designing a regime of refugee protection that is fair both to refugees and to states. There is no moral algorithm for combining contribution, benefit or capacity – and the requirements of protection vary across different types of refugee. However, drawing together the considerations that have emerged in this chapter does enable me to generate some guidelines for a fair regime:

1 States that engage in unjust conduct to another state – conduct that foreseeably generates refugees – should be held responsible for the protection of these refugees, and discharging this responsibility should not be seen as a contribution to their share of general responsibility.

2 The sharing of general responsibility should be conducted through a fair scheme of cooperation, which ensures the effective capacity of the international order of states to provide the relevant forms of refugee protection. This will require distinguishing between the *place of protection* and the *costs of protection*.

3   The place of protection of asylum refugees should be provided by states that can offer robust rights security, subject to due respect for the legitimate preferences of refugees. The sharing of responsibility for providing the place of protection – that of initial asylum and that of new membership – should acknowledge the particular salience of rights security for asylum refugees. The sharing of responsibility for providing the resettlement of asylum refugees should recognise the joint interest of the refugee and of the state of new membership in conditions of successful civic integration and the relative capacity of the political community to offer membership under a scheme in which the costs of protection are fairly shared.

4   The place of protection of sanctuary refugees should be provided by states that can (with international assistance, as required) best support the cultural and social integration of refugees. The sharing of responsibility for providing the place of protection should acknowledge the importance of aiming to match the legitimate preferences of refugees and states (given the assumption that sanctuary refugees are likely to become eligible for citizenship) and the relative capacity of states to give sanctuary under a scheme in which the costs of protection are fairly shared.

5 The place of protection of persons of refuge should be provided by states that can offer the most proximate safe spaces within which assistance (with international support as required) can be effectively delivered. The sharing of responsibility for providing the place of protection should acknowledge the relative capacity of states to offer refuge under a scheme in which the costs of protection are fairly shared.

6 The costs of protection should be initially shared on the basis of states' relative contribution to the background conditions of injustice for which they are accountable and on the basis of the relative benefit that their citizens derive from these conditions. (The initial share may be altered through free and fair responsibility exchanges between states.[11])

The translation of these points into any of several possible determinate schemes of refugee protection is a task well beyond my abilities; but they can serve as guidelines for reflection on the limitations of our current refugee regime and on reforms to this regime.

4

Predicaments of Protection

Refugee protection is a global concern and a common trust. This means that responsibility for it is shared, not individual. It also means that, unless this is shouldered widely, it may be borne by none.

Erika Feller, former UNHCR Assistant High Commissioner for Protection

Failures of Responsibility Sharing and Obligations of Solidarity

There are two central generative problems at the heart of the political challenges and ethical dilemmas confronted by the international refugee regime. The first is the ongoing reproduction of the background conditions that support the continuing production of refugees as a normal feature of our global political order. The second is the continuing failure to secure robust forms of international cooperation for sharing the responsibility for refugee protection, whether at global or at regional levels. Both of these problems make manifest the general reluctance of states to sacrifice the pursuit of their private interests or to ask their citizens to bear costs for the sake of the citizens of other states.[1] The primary focus of this chapter is on the second of these central problems and on the political challenges and ethical dilemmas that it generates for refugees, citizens and states.

Logics of Failure

An important recent report notes that 'protection, assistance, and durable solutions are provided to refugees at levels that fall well below needs, and responsibility is allocated based on proximity', before it goes on to highlight the enduring character of the issue: 'despite the fact that this state of affairs has persisted for decades, no adequate institutional mechanisms – whether legal, political, or operational – have been created to ensure more equitable and predictable responsibility-sharing'.[2]

To explain why this is the case requires noting that refugee protection exhibits features of a global public good, in the sense that the legitimacy repair work it performs is *non-excludable* (i.e. all states derive the benefit of this work towards repairing the legitimacy of the international order of states) and *non-rivalrous* (i.e. the benefits enjoyed by one state do not reduce the benefits enjoyed by other states). If we focus on this aspect of refugee protection, then it is unsurprising that it gives rise to a collective action problem, since, while all states have an interest in the global provision of refugee protection, each state has an interest in minimising its own contribution or in 'free-riding' on the work of others. This is so on account of the presumptive costs, to a state's own citizens, of providing protection, and because a state will enjoy the benefits of legitimacy work performed by others. The major constraint on states in this context is provided by the norm of non-refoulement, which makes states where refugees arrive generally reluctant to bear the reputational harm of turning them away (even where they have the capacity to do so). The effects of this logic can be seen at both regional and global levels:

- REGIONAL: The EU's Common European Asylum System was designed to assign responsibilities for refugees by distributing them between member states. It did so by way of the Dublin Regulation, which made the member state where a refugee arrived responsible for that refugee. The entirely predictable outcome of this rule, in the context of the Syrian crisis, was that member states that lay on refugee routes via the Balkans or via the Mediterranean were expected to bear the bulk of the responsibility. This led fairly rapidly to deliberate non-compliance with the rule by some states (Hungary and Italy) – and, despite several efforts to recognise the need, the EU has failed to secure its members' agreement on a fair 'quota' system of responsibility sharing.[3] The effect of this failure has been a refocused effort of making access to the EU even more difficult for refugees than it already was, by undermining and criminalising civil society actors who sought to help refugees gain entry to the EU.

- GLOBAL: Eighty-five per cent of the world's refugees are hosted in states in developing regions of the world that are proximate to refugee-producing states because, given 'their usually porous borders and strong normative obligations to offer asylum', these states 'face very little alternative other than to open their borders to refugees'. However, 'those richer states further afield face only a discretionary duty to contribute through responsibility-sharing, assuming that their access barriers work, and they are able to prevent refugees from arriving spontaneously'.[4] Hence the latter have no incentive to engage in fair responsibility sharing.

States that are unreasonably burdened by the refusal of other states to engage in fair responsibility sharing can take some steps to encourage engagement. Looking at the global context, if a southern hosting state possesses the relevant capacity, it can engage in border closure to prevent refugees from arriving, or it can enable or encourage refugees to treat it as a transit country by waving them through and thereby altering the geography of power that allows the northern states to exercise discretion. Both of these strategies have been seen in the recent Syrian refugee crisis. In 2014 Lebanon and Jordan closed their borders (with some exceptions), having accepted an estimated 1.4 million and 1.5 million refugees respectively (which amounts to a refugee to inhabitant ratio of 250 to 1,000 in Lebanon and 140 to 1,000 in Jordan) at considerable cost to their domestic economies.[5] The second strategy can be seen in the case of Turkey's waving through refugees before the EU–Turkey agreement concerning refugees, and as a way of improving its negotiating position for that agreement.[6] Two further strategies are also, although less straightforwardly or unilaterally, available: *issue linkage* and *reframing*.

Southern states can engage in issue linkage by tying refugee protection and responsibility sharing to wider international agendas, which engage the self-interest of northern states. This can take stronger (e.g. security links) and weaker (e.g. development links) forms. When southern states can make their cooperation on other issues conditional on northern states' engaging in some level of responsibility sharing, this can support a move to fairer arrangements. Engaging *reframing* involves noting another feature of refugee protection as a global public good. The relevant point here is that, while refugee protection exhibits features of a global public good, it also exhibits other features, in that the legitimacy repair benefit that it generates need not be, and often is not, the only benefit that it confers. Refugee protection can be seen as an *impure* global public good in that it, too, can give rise to benefits that are excludable or rivalrous or both.[7] Thus, for example, providing refugee protection and engaging in international cooperation for responsibility sharing can generate positive excludable and rivalrous benefits for a state in terms of its domestic self-perception and global reputation as a 'good citizen' in the international order of states (e.g. Sweden, Germany, Canada, the Netherlands) or in terms of the ideological sustenance drawn from such activity by a powerful state concerning its 'moral right' to exercise leadership in the global arena (e.g. the United States). This can help to account for the (limited) willingness of some northern states to engage in UNHCR resettlement programmes (the United States being the major resettlement location and Australia, Canada and the Nordic states also offering a significant number of places annually – significant in relation to the low total number).[8] It also helps to explain the greater than otherwise expected UNHCR funding contributions of some (typically small) states, for example the Netherlands and the Nordic states, for which the 'good citizen' mode is central to political self-perception as global political actors.[9]

The 'impure' character of refugee protection as a global public good is politically crucial because it points to the potentials of reframing as a way of pushing the contemporary circumstances of refugee protection towards securing fair responsibility sharing. To develop a case for the wider potentials of reframing, let me begin by drawing attention to three points about the argument developed in this book.

The first point is that the argument is offering a conceptual and normative *reframing* of refugee protection, of the meaning and purpose of the institution of refugeehood – namely one that ties the international refugee regime to the work of repairing legitimacy problems confronted by an international order of states whose legitimacy hangs on their claim to be able to reconcile state sovereignty and human rights. In doing so, the argument also articulates a normative conception of 'good citizenship' for states focused on the responsibility to do their fair share by securing the disposition and capacity of all states to protect, respect and fulfil at least the basic rights of their citizens and by repairing the legitimacy problems posed to this international order when any state fails to perform this task through the relevant mechanism (either the international refugee regime or the international emergency assistance regime). One reason why this frame matters is that it points to the fact that the claim of the international order of states to generate political obligations to respect state sovereignty and its expressions is conditional on the effective provision of basic rights either directly, via one's state, or reparatively, via international refugee or emergency assistance regimes. Acknowledging the conditional character of the legitimacy not only of sovereign states but also of the international order of states ties refugee protection rather more directly to the interests of states, considered both individually and collectively. A second reason is that this frame situates the issue of refugee protection within the wider terrain of legitimacy work for which states have responsibility and potentially allows for *responsibility exchanges* between states on the matter of their preferred forms of legitimacy work. This potential for flexibility in the forms of the legitimacy work undertaken by particular states also provides a basis on which states that have reasonable grounds for reluctance to engage in refugee protection can be given alternative options and held accountable against good citizenship norms.

The second point is that, in distinguishing the different claims of, and the appropriate modes of response to, three types of refugee, the argument introduces elements of a division of labour into the international refugee regime, and also provides for different (exclusive) benefits for protecting the states. The former is important because it assigns relevant criteria for distributing responsibility; but the latter is significant too. Notice, for example, that asylum calls for resettlement in a state of robust human rights protection, but it is also an act of condemnation of the persecuting state that may have particular ideological or reputational benefits for states that perceive themselves as liberal powers (e.g. the United States and the EU) – benefits that it does not have for other states. Within the normative constraints of providing the appropriate forms of refugee protection, this differentiation also allows for responsibility exchanges between states, while the distinction between *sites of protection* and *costs of protection* provides a way of holding account-able, and making alternative options available for, states that are unwilling (on reasonable grounds) or unsuitable to act as sites of protection.

The third thing to note is that there is no moral algorithm for determining fair shares of refugee protection, either overall or in relation to each of the three types of refugee, nor (we may now add) for determining fair shares of overall legitimacy work. The implication of this point is that develop-ing a scheme of refugee protection that supports fair responsibility sharing requires building institu-tional and organisational infrastructures through which determinate fair shares of responsibility can be allocated to, and assumed by, states. However, the challenge of designing a scheme that successfully motivates states to engage in fair responsibility shar-ing is a demanding one. To address the motivational problem requires at least two additional elements.

The first is providing (constrained) flexibility for states in terms of the form that their share of

responsibility for refugee protection takes by allowing for fairly negotiated responsibility exchanges
(perhaps brokered by the UNHCR) and, ideally,
by doing so within a broader framework of fair
shares of legitimacy work – one that makes room
for these exchanges across different types of such
work. Supporting justified divisions of labour
within refugee protection and facilitating legitimate
responsibility exchanges between states respects
the salience of differences between states, typically
rooted in their particular histories, in a way that
extends beyond treating states simply as *instruments*
of refugee protection. It makes space for respecting
their individuality as political communities. Such
constrained flexibility acknowledges that domestic
governments may often have politically significant
reasons for their preferred forms of legitimacy
work. Opening a route for states to co-determine,
and to present themselves to their publics as co-
determining, within the relevant constraints, the
form of their contribution reduces one of the significant incentives for non-cooperation.

The second, and related, element is promoting
good citizenship norms through tangible incentives
tied to state interests. This element points back to
the significance of issue linkage, but in a more holis-
tic manner and in relation to a more encompassing

context. Issue linkage may take varied forms. For example, across the North–South axis, cooperative responsibility sharing by states in the North could be twinned to increased cooperation from southern states around issues of security, irregular migration, preferential treatment of their companies in government contracts and of their citizens in visa arrangements – while cooperative responsibility sharing by states in the South could be twinned to additional development support in targeted areas of need, eased migration channels for their citizens, and preferential trade status. Beyond the immediate context of issue linkage, the international community could reward states that exhibit good citizenship through a preferential allocation of international roles in global institutions such as the UN, the WTO, the IMF and the World Bank, or through preferential treatments accorded by such organisations. Such a development is by no means straightforward to achieve, but we should register the grounds for a potential coalition that may work towards achieving this objective. Such a coalition would consist of many southern states that stand to benefit from the promotion of good citizenship norms in relation to refugee protection, and of a number of (typically small) northern states for which such norms have become central to political self-understanding. Achieving a scheme of international cooperation that effectively supports at least reasonably fair responsibility sharing in refugee protection is a feasible political prospect, albeit a difficult and demanding one.

State Responsibilities in Contexts of Non-Cooperation

States have a responsibility to cooperate in creating conditions of fair responsibility sharing, but what obligations arise in the absence of such cooperation? Acknowledging that there are significant gaps in the relevant data and knowledge, a recent review of the economic impact of hosting forced migrants in poor states has noted:

> In the short run, violence, environmental degradation, and disease propagation are major risks to the host populations. In the long run, infrastructure, trade, and labor markets are key channels that determine the impacts on host communities.[10]

Maystadt et al.'s (2019) study is limited to economic impacts; to answer my question, it would also need to address social and political impacts, but it already points to two general responsibilities that arise for, and fall on, the international order of states in the absence of cooperative fair sharing. One is to deal with the absence of data and knowledge. The other is to act prudently, on the basis of existing data, to support states that neighbour the refugee-producing state and are effectively coerced by this condition of non-cooperation into picking up the slack. Here that would be to mitigate the initial threats and to support developments that lead to more positive outcomes by investing in infrastructure, by enabling trade relations, and by supporting inclusive labour markets. This responsibility falls primarily on those states and organisations of states (such as the EU) that deliberately enact policies designed to frustrate fair sharing and that thereby acquire primary responsibilities to mitigate the wrong, and the consequent harms, that their actions impose on refugee-hosting states and their citizens.

This is not only a matter of responsibility to refugee-hosting states that take up the slack and to their citizens, however. There is also the responsibility to refugees who are warehoused within these states. Such a responsibility entails at least supporting capacity-building for the forms of protection – robust rights security, social integration, and emergency assistance – that are owed to refugees.

Providing these forms of support does not justify or legitimate non-cooperation but is required to mitigate its effects.

Citizen and Refugee Responsibilities in Contexts of Unfair Shares

Supporting the development of the infrastructure for international cooperation on fair responsibility sharing is a task that states, their citizens, and their refugees all are obliged to take part in. Refugees, like everyone else, have a duty to cooperate with just refugee policies and a duty to fight unjust policies (to refuse cooperation with, disobey, or resist unjust forms of, refugee governance). This duty cannot reasonably demand that they take the risks that many refugees are now taking but, as moral and political agents, refugees have duties to fight injustice where they can do so without bearing unreasonable costs. Seen from this perspective, the decision of significant numbers of refugees to undertake dangerous journeys from the state of immediate refuge to states that are well placed, but reluctant, to offer asylum and sanctuary – journeys that expose them to exploitation by unscrupulous 'transit' agents and by people smugglers, as well as to a wide range of other risks – should be viewed as an act of *transnational civil disobedience*, a refusal to be governed unjustly that extends well beyond what duty requires of them. This behaviour draws our attention to the failings of the current regime and, hence, to its inability to repair the legitimacy of the international order of states. States that deliberately choose not to support fair responsibility sharing of refugee protection – and this means pretty much all states of the global North – compromise the claim that refugees are obliged to respect their border sovereignty and weaken the normative basis of the international order more generally. Refugees may have reasons of prudence to comply with the directives of these states, but they do not have obvious reasons of political morality to do so. Refugees who act in ways that respect human rights and whose acts coerce non-cooperating states into the performance of their responsibilities are committing no wrong. We may also see the refusal of many refugees to be governed by the refugee regime in ways that do not comply with the duties owed to them as an expression of 'voice' in a regime from which their voices are largely excluded, a justified claim to inclusion in decision-making processes that give rise to the rules and norms through which, as refugees, they are governed.

What about the citizens of such non-cooperative states? In the face of the policies pursued by these states, citizens acquire duties to act in ways that support refugees – that is, duties to repair the legitimacy failure of their state (or of the regional polity, in the case of the EU). These duties may take the form of campaigning against the state's current policies, enabling the arrival of refugees, supporting their efforts to stay, or supplementing the resources available to refugees both within the state and beyond its borders. This may involve engaging in acts of non-cooperation, civil disobedience, or justified resistance to state authorities. Which actions to take where and when will be a complex matter of political judgement and will depend on the individual or collective skills, resources and capacities of the agents involved. Consider three examples.

The first is from the Netherlands:

> Taking advantage of an obscure Dutch law that forbids the police to interrupt church services, ministers at Bethel Church in The Hague had been running a round-the-clock liturgy since October 26th in order to prevent the five members of the Tamrazyan family from being arrested and sent back to Armenia. Pastors from across Europe visited Bethel to participate in the service, many with several members of their congregations in tow,

while more than 250,000 people signed a petition calling for a change to the law under which hundreds of families like the Tamrazyans could have been deported.[11]

Here the use of a legal norm combined with the ability to mobilise a specific constituency of actors supported a practice of obstructing the state's unreasonable attempt to deport refugees. This is an example of justified non-cooperation.

The second example is that of the Stansted 15 in the United Kingdom. A group of activists engaged in a deliberate act of law breaking by preventing aircraft engaged in carrying out unjust deportations from taking off, and did so in a way that inconvenienced but did not endanger others. The police initially charged the group with aggravated trespassing, which is an offence carrying a maximum three-month custodial sentence. This was an entirely legitimate act of civil disobedience and appropriately treated as such by the police. (By contrast, the government's decision to charge the activists with the far more serious offence of intentional disruption of services at an aerodrome – an offence said to pose a 'real and material' risk to the airport – was a deliberate attempt to 'chill' a legitimate protest; and it was accurately described by the NGO Liberty as a 'malicious attack' on the right to peaceful protest.[12])

The third example is an imagined one. A recent report notes:

> As a donor, through direct institutional involvement, and by providing a mission framework for Member States, the EU has established a strategy of externalised obstruction of asylum that is contributing to the complete containment of asylum-seekers in a situation of fundamental rightlessness in Libya.[13]

This is an illegitimate (and, arguably, also illegal)[14] policy. Suppose, then, that an activist organisation chose to address Europe's policy by establishing an 'underground railway' that enables significant numbers of those who seek refugee status to gain relatively safe access to the territory of the EU – at which point they become directly subject to the norm of non-refoulement. The activities of such an organisation are likely to be in breach of numerous national and EU laws, but would they represent a legitimate form of justified resistance? Under current conditions, it is hard to see why this would not be so, because such activities would enable refugees to exercise their rights and would coerce the EU into performing its duty, and this is not to wrong the EU.[15]

In both the EU and the United States today we witness increasing efforts to criminalise active support for refugees.[16] This can, I think, be conceived of as a manifestation of governmental *bad conscience* – an acknowledgement that the work of citizens in supporting refugees draws unwelcome attention to their own legitimacy failures. I began this book with the stories of two ships, MS *St Louis* and MV *Aquarius*. What followed the doomed voyage of the former should remind us that the fate of the latter is a warning signal of the potential emergence of a world in which the reconciliation of state sovereignty and human rights ceases to be a matter of political concern, in which human rights are sacrificed on the altar of a far-right nationalist vision of state sovereignty. The possibility of such a development should matter to states, citizens, and refugees alike.

Notes

Notes to Prologue

1 United States Holocaust Memorial Museum, 'Voyage of the St Louis'. https://encyclopedia.ushmm.org/content/en/article/voyage-of-the-st-louis.

2 Ibid.

3 Ibid.

4 Ibid.

5 Ibid.

6 'Italy's Matteo Salvini Shuts Ports to Migrant Rescue Ship'. https://www.bbc.co.uk/news/world-europe-44432056.

7 'MSF Ship *Aquarius* Ends Migrant Rescues in Mediterranean'. https://www.bbc.co.uk/news/world-europe-46477158.

8 Visit https://missingmigrants.iom.int/region/mediterranean.

Notes to Introduction

1 Kelly Oliver (2017) refers to this warehousing as 'carceral humanitarianism'.
2 Parekh (2017) provides a detailed analysis of this problem.
3 The case of the European Union – the regional body perhaps best placed to engage in such cooperative practices between states – demonstrates that securing such cooperation is extremely difficult to achieve. Rather than coordinated refugee protection, the EU has witnessed a crisis of integration and a resurgence of nationalist populisms, of which Italy's Matteo Salvini is simply one manifestation.
4 The final draft of the Compact can be found here: https://www.unhcr.org/events/conferences/5b3295167/ official-version-final-draft-global-compact-refugees. html. This agreement was adopted on 17 December 2018. Only two states voted against it – the United States and Hungary.
5 Cherem (2016), p. 185.
6 Betts and Collier (2017), p. 99; this marks a significant contrast with Betts (2013).
7 Cherem (2016), p. 191.
8 Cherem (2016), p. 191, citing Walzer (1983), pp. 44–5 and 48.
9 Visit https://www.unhcr.org/figures-at-a-glance.html.
10 Visit https://www.unhcr.org/5baa00b24.
11 Visit https://www.unhcr.org/globaltrends2017.
12 See Fitzgerald (2019) for a detailed analysis.
13 For some reflections on this topic, see Gibney (2015).

14 My approach here is influenced by Shue (1995), Beitz (2009) and Sangiovanni (2016).
15 This phrase trades off the analogy with *in loco parentis*; for an initial formulation, see Owen (2016b).

Notes to Chapter 1

1 Haddad (2008), p. 59; see also Soguk (1999).
2 Orchard (2014), p. 1.
3 Ibid.
4 Ibid., pp. 71–104.
5 Ibid., p. 102. Asylum was seen as part of the 'standards of civilisation' by which European-based international socicty defined itself and that, it should be stressed, were mobilised as justification for members of this political order to engage in imperialist interventions outside their domain.
6 Ibid., p. 102.
7 Gatrell (2013), pp. 22–4.
8 Ibid., p. 49.
9 Ibid., pp. 49–50.
10 Ibid., p. 49.
11 Ibid., p. 55.
12 Ibid.
13 Orchard (2014), pp. 114–16.
14 Ibid., pp. 116–17.
15 League of Nations, *Convention concerning the Status of Refugees Coming from Germany*, 10 February 1938. League of Nations Treaty Series, vol. 192, No. 4461, p. 59. http://www.refworld.org/docid/3dd8d12a4.html.

16 Orchard (2014), p. 117.

17 Gatrell (2013), p. 109.

18 There were two exceptions to the scope of UNHCR for refugee protection relating to Palestine/Israel and Korea. See Akram (2014) for pertinent discussion.

19 Visit http://www.refugeelegalaidinformation.org/19 51-convention for the 1951 Convention, Article 1 A (2) and the 1967 Protocol, Article 1 (2).

20 See Feller et al. (2003), pp.178–9, and Goodwin-Gill and Adam (2007), p. 201 for more detailed specifications concerning the duty of non-refoulement.

21 See the 1951 Convention, especially Articles 13–30.

22 Keely (1996), p. 1057, cited in Martin (2014), p. 82.

23 Loescher (2001), pp. 82–7.

24 Ibid., pp. 112–13.

25 Ibid., p. 113.

26 Ibid.

27 Martin (2014), pp. 89–90; see also Hathaway (2007).

28 Martin (2014), p. 90; see also Adelman and McGrath (2007).

29 See Feller et al. (2003) for an overview of these developments.

30 McAdam (2014), pp. 204–5.

31 Ibid., p. 209.

32 Ibid.

Notes to Chapter 2

1 Shacknove (1985), p. 276.

2 Ibid.

3 Ibid., p. 275.

4 Ibid., p. 277.
5 Ibid., p. 281; see pp. 278–81 for the full argument. Shacknove is here drawing on Shue's (1995) discussion of basic rights but, perhaps given the humanitarian impetus of his argument, reconstrues this in terms of basic needs and what is essential to survival.
6 Shacknove (1985), p. 282.
7 Ibid.
8 Ibid., p. 277. This analytic separation, it seems to me, stands in tension with Shue's argument, especially as elaborated in Shue (1995).
9 Gibney (2004), p. 7.
10 Ibid., p. 8.
11 Price (2009), p. 73.
12 Ibid.
13 Ibid.
14 See Owen (2016a, 2018).
15 See Hindess (1998, 2003).
16 This argument could also be developed in terms of the collective responsibility of participants in a scheme of cooperation designed to ensure conditions of background justice through the construction of a just basic structure.
17 More precisely, it does so if we grant the practical possibility of a regime of global governance in which these basic rights can be universally protected.
18 This type of argument is given fuller development in Brock forthcoming.
19 Carens (2013), p. 196.
20 Whether establishing such 'safe havens' is a prudent move or not is a distinct question; the

salient point here is simply to register a conceptual difference between alienage and *in loco civitatis*, in that the latter does not rule out that the institution of refugeehood applies to persons in such safe havens.

21 The case of a refugee from a state that is incapable of protection is, I think, better placed under the category of sanctuary than under that of asylum. I am grateful to Matt Gibney for urging me to clarify this point.

22 Price (2009), p. 248.

23 David Miller contends: 'it seems wrong to single out those who are escaping persecution and grant them permanent residence immediately on the grounds that having arrived they will all choose to identify politically with the society that takes them in' (Miller 2016, pp. 135–6). This response misses the point of the argument that Price and Cherem are advancing.

24 Persecution can take many forms, including denial of citizenship to persons entitled to that status. Unfortunately exploring this issue in depth is beyond the scope of this book.

25 I discuss this in the next chapter.

26 Gibney (2015), p. 459.

27 Owen (2013), p. 334.

28 See Owen (2013) for such an argument.

29 Note that these considerations only indicate that non-voluntary repatriation is not ruled out as a matter of principle by a grant of sanctuary; but they are not sufficient to justify non-voluntary repatriation, as

this would require consideration of wider issues of just conditions of return.

30 In this respect, it does not cover non-discrete events such as climate change, although it may certainly cover specific discrete events that are effects of climate change.

31 See the Cartagena Declaration on Refugees at https://www.oas.org/dil/1984_cartagena_declaration_on_re fugees.pdf.

Notes to Chapter 3

1 Important work on asylum as reparation has been done by Souter (2014a and 2014b); my argument may be seen, in part, as an extension and expansion of his work.

2 See Owen 2016c for a fuller defence of this view.

3 See Bauböck (2017).

4 Visit https://drc.ngo/media/4167496/drc-diaspora-programme_study_syrian-diaspora-groups-in-eur ope_web.pdf for an overview of their salience.

5 See Jones and Teytelboym (2016); also Jones and Teytelboym (n.d., published online, at http://www.europarl.europa.eu/cmsdata/109080/The_refugee_match.pdf) and Owen (2018b), pp. 36–40.

6 Carens (2013), ch. 8 and Rubio-Marin (2000).

7 For an overview, see Hammond (2014) and Crisp and Long (2016). The best treatment is Bradley (2013), but see also Gerver (2018).

8 See Amnesty International 2017 at https://www.am nesty.org/download/Documents/ASA1168662017

ENGLISH.PDF (the text is titled *Forced Back to Danger: Asylum-Seekers Returned from Europe to Afghanistan*).

9 See Parekh (2017) for pertinent observations.

10 There are two further points to notice here. First, in practice, these special obligations of states to refugees for whose situation they are (in significant part) responsible will typically also entail obligations of the same states to the states in which the refugees seek immediate safety and who thereby incur costs for which the outcome-responsible states are accountable. Second, there are two important conditions under which special obligations are not generated even if the actions of external states played a significant causal role in producing the refugee flow. The first condition is satisfied in cases where the outcome is not reasonably foreseeable. The second condition has particular salience for cases of sanctuary and hangs on the legitimacy of the actions of the relevant states, specifically on whether these actions are authorised under the norms of the international order of states and hence can be seen to be consonant with, or representative of, this international order.

11 I develop this point in the next chapter.

Notes to Chapter 4

1 Addressing the first would contribute to addressing the second, in that a reduction in the demand for, and overall costs of, refugee protection is likely to lower the perceived risks of cooperation. Addressing

the second may, however, also contribute to addressing the first, if refugees, while enjoying that status and after they no longer require it, are integrated into transnational development policies.

2 Betts, Costello, and Zaun (2017), p. 16.

3 See Bauböck (2017) for a salient discussion.

4 Betts et al. (2017), p. 30.

5 Visit http://arabcenterdc.org/policy_analyses/syrian-refugees-in-jordan-and-lebanon-the-politics-of-their-return.

6 Betts et al. (2017), p. 32, drawing on Greenhill (2016).

7 See Betts (2003).

8 Visit https://www.unhcr.org/resettlement.html.

9 In support of this claim, see Betts (2003), pp. 283–6.

10 Maystadt et al. (2019).

11 Visit https://www.irishtimes.com/news/world/europe/three-month-dutch-church-vigil-to-protect-refugees-finally-ends-1.3777301.

12 Visit https://www.theguardian.com/uk-news/2018/dec/10/activists-convicted-of-terror-offence-for-blocking-stansted-deportation-flight.

13 Reyhani et al. (2019), p. 13.

14 Ibid., p. 15, n. 170.

15 For pertinent reflections on justified resistance, see Delmas (2018).

16 The case of Scott Warren is indicative: visit https://www.npr.org/2019/05/28/725716169/extending-zero-tolerance-to-people-who-help-migrants-along-the-border?t=1559134974052.

References

Adelman, H. and McGrath, S. 2007. 'To Date or to Marry: That Is the Question'. *Journal of Refugee Studies* 20: 376–80.

Akram, S. 2014. 'UNRWA and Palestinian Refugees'. In *The Oxford Handbook of Refugee and Forced Migration Studies*, edited by E. Fiddian-Qasmiyeh, G. Loescher, K. Long and N. Sigona. Oxford: Oxford University Press, 227–40.

Bauböck, R. 2017. *Democratic Inclusion*. Manchester: Manchester University Press.

Beitz, C. 2009. *The Idea of Human Rights*. Oxford: Oxford University Press.

Betts, A. 2003. 'Public Goods Theory and the Provision of Refugee Protection: The Role of the Joint Product Model in Burden-Sharing Theory'. *Journal of Refugee Studies* 16 (3): 274–96.

Betts, A. 2009. *Forced Migration and Global Politics*. Oxford: Wiley Blackwell.

Betts, A. 2013. *Survival Migration: Failed Governance*

and the Crisis of Displacement. Ithaca, NY: Cornell University Press.

Betts, A. and Collier, P. 2017. *Refuge: Transforming a Broken Refugee System.* London: Penguin.

Betts, A., Costello, C. and Zaun, N. 2017. *A Fair Share: Refugees and Responsibility Sharing.* Delmi Report. http://www.delmi.se/en/publications-seminars#!/en/a-fair-share-refugees-and-responsibility-sharing-report-and-policy-brief-201710.

Bradley, M. 2013. *Refugee Repatriation: Justice, Responsibility and Redress.* Cambridge: Cambridge University Press.

Brock, G. forthcoming. *Justice for People on the Move: Migration in Challenging Times.* London: Bloomsbury Academic.

Carens, J. 2013. *The Ethics of Immigration.* Oxford: Oxford University Press.

Cherem, M. 2016. 'Refugee Rights: Against Expanding the Definition of a "Refugee" and Unilateral Protection Elsewhere'. *Journal of Political Philosophy* 24 (2): 183–205.

Crisp, J. and Long, K. 2016. 'Safe and Voluntary Refugee Repatriation: From Principle to Practice'. *Journal on Migration and Human Security* 4 (3): 141–5.

Delmas, C. 2018. *A Duty to Resist: When Disobedience Should Be Uncivil.* Oxford: Oxford University Press.

Feller, E., Türk, V. and Nicholson, F. 2003. *Refugee Protection in International Law: UNHCR's Global Consultations on International Protection.* Cambridge: Cambridge University Press. https://www.unhcr.org/uk/

protection/globalconsult/4a1ba1aa6/refugee-protec
tion-international-law.html.

Fitzgerald, D. S. 2019. *Refuge beyond Reach: How Rich Democracies Repel Asylum Seekers*. Oxford: Oxford University Press.

Gatrell, P. 2013. *The Making of the Modern Refugee*. Oxford: Oxford University Press.

Gerver, M. 2018. *The Ethics and Practice of Refugee Repatriation*. Edinburgh: Edinburgh University Press.

Gibney, M. J. 2004. *The Ethics and Politics of Asylum: Liberal Democracy and the Response to Refugees*. Cambridge: Cambridge University Press.

Gibney, M. J. 2015. 'Refugees and Justice Between States'. *European Journal of Political Theory* 14 (4): 448–63.

Goodwin-Gill, G. S. and McAdam, J. 2007. *The Refugee in International Law*. Oxford: Oxford University Press.

Greenhill, K. M. 2016. 'Open Arms behind Barred Doors: Fear, Hypocrisy, and Policy Schizophrenia in the European Migration Crisis'. *European Law Journal* 22 (3): 317–32.

Haddad, E. 2008. *The Refugee in International Society: Between Sovereigns*. Cambridge: Cambridge University Press.

Hammond, L. 2014. '"Voluntary" Repatriation and Reintegration'. In *The Oxford Handbook of Refugee and Forced Migration Studies*, edited by E. Fiddian-Qasmiyeh, G. Loescher, K. Long and N. Sigona. Oxford: Oxford University Press, 499–511.

References

Hathaway, J. 2007. 'Forced Migration Studies: Could We Agree Just to "Date"?'. *Journal of Refugee Studies* 20: 349–69.

Hindess, B. 1998. 'Divide and Rule: The International Character of Modern Citizenship'. *European Journal of Social Theory* 1 (1): 57–70.

Hindess, B. 2003. 'Responsibility for Others in the Modern System of States'. *Journal of Sociology* 39 (1): 23–30.

Jones, W. and Teitelboym, A. 2016. 'Choice, Preferences, and Priorities in a Matching System for Refugees'. *Forced Migration Review* 51: 80–2.

Jones, W. and Teitelboym, A. n.d. 'The Refugee Match'. European Parliament. http://www.europarl.europa.eu/cmsdata/109080/The_refugee_match.pdf.

Keely, C. 1996. 'How Nation-States Create and Respond to Refugee Flows'. *International Migration Review* 20 (4): 1046–66.

Loescher, G. 2001. *The UNHCR and World Politics: A Perilous Path*. Oxford: Oxford University Press.

McAdam, J. 2014. 'Human Rights and Forced Migration'. In *The Oxford Handbook of Refugee and Forced Migration Studies*, edited by E. Fiddian-Qasmiyeh, G. Loescher, K. Long and N. Sigona. Oxford: Oxford University Press, 203–14.

Martin, S. 2014. *International Migration: Evolving Trends from the Early Twentieth Century to the Present*. Cambridge: Cambridge University Press.

Maystadt, J.-F., Hirvonen, K., Mabiso, A. and Vandercasteelen, J. 2019. 'Impacts of Hosting Forced Migrants in Poor Countries'. *Annual*

Review of Resource Economics 11, doi: 10.1146/annurev-resource-090518-095629.

Miller, D. 2016. *Strangers in Our Midst: The Political Philosophy of Immigration*. Cambridge, MA: Harvard University Press.

Oliver, K. 2017. *Carceral Humanitarianism: Logics of Refugee Detention*. Minneapolis: University of Minnesota Press.

Orchard, P. 2014. *The Right to Flee: Refugees, States and the Construction of International Cooperation*. Cambridge: Cambridge University Press.

Owen, D. 2013. 'Citizenship and the Marginalities of Migrants'. *Critical Review in Social and Political Philosophy* 16 (3): 326–43.

Owen, D. 2016a. 'Citizenship and Human Rights'. In *The Oxford Handbook of Citizenship*, edited by A. Shachar, R. Bauboeck, I. Bloemraad and M. Vink. Oxford: Oxford University Press, 247–66.

Owen, D. 2016b. '*In loco civitatis*: On the Normative Structure of Refugeehood and the International Refugee Regime'. In *Migration in Political Theory*, edited by S. Fine and L. Ypi. Oxford: Oxford University Press, 269–90.

Owen, D. 2016c. 'Refugees, Fairness and Taking up the Slack'. *Moral Philosophy and Politics* 3 (2): 141–64.

Owen, D. 2018a. 'On the Right to Have Nationality Rights: Statelessness, Citizenship and Human Rights'. *Netherlands International Law Review* 65: 299–317.

Owen, D. 2018b. 'Refugees and Shared Responsibilities of Justice'. *Global Justice* 11 (1): 23–44.

References

Parekh, S. 2017. *Refugees and the Ethics of Forced Displacement*. London: Routledge.

Price, M. 2009. *Rethinking Asylum: History, Purpose, Limits*. Cambridge: Cambridge University Press.

Reyhani, A.-N., del Tronco, C. G. and Mayer, M. N. 2019. 'Challenging the Externalised Obstruction of Asylum: The Application of the Right to Asylum to EU Cooperation with Libyan Coast Guards'. https://papers.ssrn.com/sol3/papers.cfm?abstract_id=3361889.

Rubio-Marin, R. 2000. *Immigration as a Democratic Challenge*. Cambridge: Cambridge University Press.

Sangiovanni, A. 2016. 'How Practices Matter'. *Journal of Political Philosophy* 24 (1): 3–23.

Shacknove, A. E. 1985. 'Who Is a Refugee?'. *Ethics* 95 (2): 274–84.

Shue, H. 1995. *Basic Rights: Subistence, Affluence and US Foreign Policy*. Princeton, NJ: Princeton University Press.

Soguk, N. 1999. *States and Strangers: Refugees and the Displacements of Statecraft*. Minnesota: University of Minnesota Press.

Souter, J. 2014a. 'Durable Solutions as Reparation for the Unjust Harms of Displacement: Who Owes What to Refugees?'. *Journal of Refugee Studies* 27 (2): 171–90.

Souter, J. 2014b. 'Towards a Theory of Asylum as Reparation for Past Injustice'. *Political Studies* 62 (2): 326–42.

Walzer, M. 1983. *Spheres of Justice: A Defense of Pluralism and Equality*. New York: Basic Books.